# RETURN
## TO
# RADIANCE

# RETURN
## TO
# RADIANCE

### A 21 DAY
### TRANSFORMATION
### TO VITALITY

Susan Taylor, Ph.D.

Center for Meditation Science

**Center for Meditation Science, Inc.**
99 Grimms Road
Honesdale, Pennsylvania 18431
SusanTaylor.org

*Cover & Interior Design:* Joan Greenblatt (CenterPointeMedia.com)
*Editor:* Jagati (Jagati1word@gmail.com)
*Editor:* Heidi L. Audet (heidiaudet@gmail.com)
*Illustrations:* Samrat Chakraborty (samratchakraborty333@gmail.com)

ISBN: 978-0-9768291-9-5
Library of Congress Control Number: 2020912509

# Table of Contents

# Part II: Decoding Lessons from the East

# Part III: A Total Program for Radiance

## CHAPTER 12
**The Healing Power of Meditation**.............................232

# Part IV: The Start-Up 21-Day Plan

# Part V: Appendices

# Preface

*We will find our way to greater fulfillment through having the vitality to focus on our life's purpose. Everyone can experience their extraordinary potential that so yearns to be fulfilled and expressed.*

As I reflect on my personal journey through life, I contemplate the intentions that motivated me to write and teach for the last four decades. I recall that after writing and publishing my first book, I was caught in the whirlwind of "self-promotion," with all of the radio, television, public appearances, and book signings. At the very same time, I was invited to go on a trip to Mt. Kailash in Tibet. I recall the moment I heard about the trip, I was filled with inspiration. I prepared myself to meet the Himalayas and sold many of my belongings to make the trip possible. I was going on a pilgrimage. The burning desire to experience my innermost self gave me courage to move past the obstacles that came my way. All of the challenges I met helped me to climb the summit of my own fear and self-doubt. The journey was truly transformative.

After my second journey to the mountaintop, I felt inspired to serve, and to teach what I had received from the masters of the Himalayan Tradition. I wrote several books and directed programs over the next few years.

As I originally intended, I now spend my time teaching practical strategies rooted in ancient practices and modern science to those seeking self-tranformation.

The purpose of *Return to Radiance* serves this very moment in time. People want and need authentic knowledge, skills, and practices to reclaim their true intelligent potential and brilliance. We all have the desire to be seen, heard and understood. We will find our way to greater fulfillment through having the vitality to focus on our life's purpose. With skill, precision, and systematic practice, everyone can experience their extraordinary potential that so yearns to be fulfilled and expressed.

*Return to Radiance* reflects my desire to share with you the knowledge and practices I have been fortunate to receive. May it provide you with the wisdom to walk in the light of your full potential and transform that essence into effulgent vitality.

# Introduction

*Vitality is our birthright. Set yourself up for success by developing self-awareness. It is here, inside yourself and nowhere else, where you will find the key to your inner radiance.*

I have spent most of my life studying myself as I navigated my ups and downs. Like everyone else, I have met the challenges of self doubt and fear in my life. I have lived in many places, teaching and advising, working as a medical scientist, and even training the four leggeds.

All of the experiences I have gained through life brought me where I am today with no regret; instead, a profound awareness of the forces that helped guide me to be healthy and happy. My experiences have shown me that health and happiness are dynamic, and require all of us to journey within rather than search outside of ourselves for the answers. If we aspire to "be radiant," access to our inner dimensions is essential. When we access all dimensions of ourselves, we are able to integrate the physical, emotional and spiritual aspects of ourselves. We can eat, breathe, and focus our mind with ease, which enables us to harness the healing force that returns us to radiance. *Return to Radiance* is a book that can guide you in restoring your life force, your vitality and with it, your self-confidence, optimism, and the joy of living. The teachings here are based on yoga science combined with and supported by the most recent discoveries in cutting-edge science. We can learn how to improve the quality of our life, beyond our financial and professional status, by establishing some healthy habits through these tried and tested practices.

The *Return to Radiance* program you'll find in this book is culled from my own experience, and backed by my training in nutritional biochemistry, meditation science, and Traditional Chinese and Ayurvedic Medicines. Many of the women I have worked with have regained their energy, vitality, and *joie de vivre;* they have returned to "radiance."

My intention is that you will also, through the simple, but profound steps laid out in the following chapters. You will become familiar with the way your body, breath, and mind all work together as you move through the book. It offers a structured program to ignite energy and vitality, so that you can carry out your best intentions.

Your new regimen will soon begin yielding tangible benefits. You'll start feeling better within days of beginning this program, and from there, the improvements will only grow. If you continue with it, I can assure you that this proven whole-body program will show you the way to reach the very zenith of energy and rejuvenation, your inner radiance.

## HOW TO USE THIS BOOK

*Return to Radiance* contains a guide for positive change to revitalize your body, mind, and spirit. Here you'll learn how to heal, nourish, and transform yourself at every level, by using food, herbs, supplements, breathing exercises, movement, and meditation. All of these resources and techniques work synergistically, although incorporating even one or two into your present life will yield benefits. The habits of a lifetime we have created—good, or not so good—aren't changed overnight. That is why you'll find supportive exercises and practices in the last section of the book. They are carefully designed to give you the tools you need to uncover and cultivate positive change at your own pace. Feel free to go back to any previous chapter if you think you've missed an important connection, or if you've lost touch with the inspiration that propelled you into the practices you have discovered.

There is no formula that works for everyone. Although the principles and strategies laid out in this book apply to all of us, you're the only one who knows how to adapt them to your own situation and needs. Keep yourself in balance by paying attention to what works for you. Remember that you are an individual with a unique biochemistry. Therefore, I recommend acquiring a blank book or journal that you can use to record your explorations with the exercises. You'll find it illuminating and productive to consult previous notes when you engage in new exercises, and to read back over the notes after completing the entire program. You will gain valuable insights about what worked best for you.

The most important practice underlying all the exercises and techniques you'll find in this program is simply the art of *paying attention*. Given our current culture of busyness, many of us have little awareness of what is happening inside of ourselves. Yet, the wellspring of unending positive transformation and vitality lies right here, within the heart of our experiences. The only requirement is for us to be present. The practices offered in this book ultimately point to the same truth: you already have the solution inside you to overcome fatigue, frustration, anxiety, depression, and what society deems to be "age-related" loss of function. To discover your inner solution, you need to bring your attention to your own experience.

Remember, vitality is our birthright. I encourage you to set yourself up for success by developing self-awareness. It is here, inside yourself and nowhere else, where you will find the key to your inner radiance.

# PART I

# The Metabolic Connection

# CHAPTER 1

─────────○─────────

# The Mystery of Radiance

*Radiance is the* inner luminosity *or brilliance
which occurs when we are energetic and* **vital;**
*it occurs when our inner light is bright.*

I've had a passion for many things over the years. I dearly love Bach and the Beatles, independence, mountain-climbing—and most of all, self-exploration. But over the past forty years, one steady fascination or passion, if you will, has held firm. I've studied it from all sides, taught it, and examined its workings in my own life, every single day. This overriding passion of mine is to understand the workings of the mind; what I refer to as *the mind's metabolism.*

The clinical term *metabolism* tends to make people's eyes glaze over. Once we can move past this temporary obstacle, though, we get to the term's real meaning. The mind's metabolism is our inner fire—our radiance, that luminous vital energy that dwells within us. It's literally the crucible of life and death, and it's at the heart of both the problem and the solution. Depending on the health of the mind's metabolism, it can bring us to the mountaintop—or pull us down to the depths of discouragement and despair.

We can't live at our full capacity unless this inner fire is being fed, focused and contained. Our contemporary lifestyle, however, seems designed to dampen our inner fire, thus depleting our vitality. Consequently, too many of us are diminishing the living spark required to live our best life. This state of affairs manifests in poor physical health, mental turmoil, and spiritual unrest.

## WHAT IS RADIANCE?

When I ask people, "Do you want to be radiant?" Everyone always says, "Yes, of course!" What does it actually mean to be radiant, though? Is it the way you feel at twenty? Does it come from doing work you love? Does radiance depend on looking sexually attractive or having a good relationship?

All of these circumstances can help put us in touch with our radiance, but true radiance is not dependent on age or circumstances.

Radiance is the *inner luminosity* or brilliance which occurs when we are energetic and **vital;** it occurs when our inner light is bright. The word vitality comes from the Latin word *vita*, meaning "life." It's the life force with which we were born. To be vital is to be in touch with that natural wellspring of renewable positive energy; the condition of that wellspring of vitality is dependent upon what we do to feed and nurture it. When we are healthy in mind and body, it shows in the outward expression of our radiance. The stronger our life energy, the more radiance we exude.

It is inevitable that we are going to get older. How we age is determined to some degree by our genetic makeup. However, a far more important influence is our everyday lifestyle habits—how we eat, how we breathe, how we move and most importantly, how we think.

These patterns are so familiar and comfortable that most of us don't even recognize them as habits. We think of them as facets of our personality—inherent and inescapable. In reality, however, the unhealthy and unhelpful patterns we've established through-out our lives are acquired behaviors that have become so deeply ingrained in us that we've come to identify with them.

We can unlearn the habits that drain our vitality. When we do, we become the architects of our own lives. This is a much brighter and more dynamic approach to "the normal course of aging." Best of all, it's totally realistic.

Arabian legend reveres the Phoenix, a mythical bird that was consumed by fire every five hundred years. After the fire died down, a new, young phoenix would spring from the ashes. In the mythology of ancient Egypt, the Phoenix represented the sun, which dies at night and is reborn in the morning. Early Christian tradition adopted the Phoenix as a symbol of both immortality and resurrection. When a myth keeps surfacing in various cultures, and over centuries as this one has, we know that there must be some kernel of truth in it, something that human beings everywhere instinctively recognize as a reflection of their own inner experience. When I first read the legend of The Phoenix, I made a copy of it and put it on the wall. It activated some inner knowing for me, that challenged all those gloomy messages we as a society are bombarded with regarding the aging process.

The truth at the heart of the phoenix story is this: each of us has the power to rejuvenate our own body, mind, and spirit.

## WHY DO WE LOSE OUR BRILLIANCE?

According to physiologists, we should be able to live for as long as two hundred years. Why, then, do we lose our brilliance? What happens? Furthermore, why in our own culture does the aging process trigger such precipitous and dramatic declining changes in our physical and mental functioning?

These questions were the impetus that fueled my self-inquiry for healing and transformation. Have you ever noticed how some people seem to resign themselves to fatigue, and depression, as if it is their natural destiny? I couldn't believe this to be true, so I made my mind up. It was time to crack the code of the pervasive anxiety, fatigue and depression related to aging and loss of vitality I was witnessing in a good number of my clients. Through my studies in nutritional biochemistry, Traditional Chinese Medicine, and Ayurvedic Medicine—the ancient Indian science of rejuvenation—my suspicions were confirmed. The dismal warnings I'd been bombarded with were based more on fear and ignorance than reality.

As the legend of the Phoenix demonstrates, we have the ability within our own being to rejuvenate ourselves, again and again.

What do I mean by *return to radiance*? I mean that it is possible to bring our mind back home to our body and rediscover our luminous, vital font of energy that originates from within. When we return to our radiance, we enhance the quality of both our physical body and our mind. These changes stimulate a transformation in our quality of life. This is no esoteric pipe dream: we've all interacted with this feeling, probably several times in our lives.

Take the experience of falling in love. Remember how that felt? Did you eat and sleep a lot? Were you fearful about the future? Or, were you enthusiastic, encouraged, joyful, full of peace, and looking forward to the next moment? That positive, enlivened, vibrant feeling is a natural consequence when there is a free flow of vital energy.

That glorious "in love" feeling doesn't last though. Not because our vital energy dies, but because we've attributed it to an *external source*. No external source, regardless of how magical, wonderful, or authentic, can equal or sustain the radiance that arises naturally within ourselves. So we blame our lover for changing, or we blame ourselves for not being able to stay in love, and we slip back into our narrow, devitalized, everyday existence.

The source of our vitality is always available to us. We can tap into it daily, whether or not we are externally supported, loved or acknowledged.

————○————

Unfortunately, the current climate of our Western culture does not fully encourage bringing our mind back "home." In fact, the antithesis of this predominates. We are conditioned to believe that our source of vitality and happiness is outside of us. We're moving way too fast to even recognize what is happening. We don't have enough hours in the day to get our work done, and we don't make the time to nourish our bodies. Instead of supporting radiance, our world currently seems to be set up for systematic isolation and degeneration. The fundamental principles governing human health and well-being are breaking down. So we go looking for a magic bullet: the drug, a belief system, a healing modality, the relationship, or a diet that will miraculously fix all our physical and mental discomfort and make us more beautiful, more brilliant.

If such a magic bullet had been found, we'd all be free of anxiety and illness (and somebody would be very, very rich!). The band-aid, quick-fix approach can't sustain long-term energy and vitality. Repeatedly falling back on caffeine, pharmaceuticals, and adrenaline rushes steadily weakens both body and mind. The "fix" is imaginary.

Our body's true energy source is internal. No external solution for inner uneasiness can ever address the source of our energy drain. It can only offer temporary symptomatic relief. Immediate, short-term respite can sometimes be exactly what the situation calls for; however, as a long-term strategy the quick fix rapidly reaches the point of diminishing returns.

Fortunately we have options. We have choices that don't necessarily require us to quit our jobs, give up our cars, or leave our families. We can rekindle our vital energy right in the midst of our fast-paced lifestyles. All it takes is a clear understanding of the underlying forces that have brought us to where we are, and a *genuine* willingness to strike out on a new path of vibrant health and clarity—radiance.

————◯————

I often encounter people who have undertaken a sincere spiritual journey. These seekers deeply long to go beyond the conventional limitations of their own human potential. All too often, though, no matter how powerful their resolve, they soon find their motivation and momentum faltering. They might ask, "Why can't I follow through?" Some will say, "I just don't seem to have the willpower, discipline or endurance."

As I studied my own experience, it became clear to me that my spiritual growth is inextricably linked to the health and wellness of my mind and body. Our body draws its nourishment from our lifelong physical and mental habits. If those habits are depleting our energy and vitality, spiritual progress will grind to a halt.

Many of these habits may seem benign on the surface. However, the cumulative effects on our bodies and minds over years can be depleting. Although the spiritual path can sometimes feel noble and transcendent, we will inevitably hit a roadblock unless we're willing and able to recognize and revise our devitalizing lifestyle habits.

When the body is in pain, the mind is forced to focus on bodily functions. If the energy in your body is not flowing in a healthy way, or if it's creating obstacles, your mind remains at the level of coping with your physical condition. A disturbed mind affects your entire being—when the body is out of balance, the mind cannot be clear. The mind will not be free to move toward higher levels of consciousness where the experiences of joy and peace await us. Meanwhile, when it comes to our everyday functioning, we cannot operate fully at any level. This leaves us vulnerable to dis-ease—or what society generally believes is "the normal course of aging."

The good news is that we have everything we need right now to start making the changes that will set us on a vibrant path to physical, mental, emotional, and spiritual transformation.

———————◯———————

How does one return to radiance? On the physical level. It all begins with metabolic regulation. Our metabolism governs the mechanics of how we move, how our organs function, how we breathe, and how we think. When my clients say, "My metabolism is sluggish," they're essentially telling me that their energy is low.

As I've said, vital energy is linked with our life force—the essence of being. We're in touch with that essence when we feel totally at peace and centered. We are radiant. It's a positive feedback loop: peacefulness and centeredness nourish a healthy essence, from which further peace and centeredness flow.

I would ask you these important questions: "What is your purpose in life? Is it to somehow make it through the days with as little effort and discomfort as possible? Is it to make yourself look better, or to own things?" Even if these are your true goals, having your energy and vitality at peak performance will make them more easily attainable.

If, however, your purpose is to discover your unique gift—your calling, if you will—and find a way to offer it to the world, then cultivating your vital energy is essential. It's an absolute prerequisite for living the full and joyous life you've always known is possible. It is the key ingredient for being radiant.

In the following chapters, I am going to be specific about the proper foods to eat, what exercises to do, and what breathing practices you will want to establish in order to build a foundation for mind/body energy and rejuvenation. The end of the book will conclude with a three-week program for radiance seekers to begin their journey. It is created to bring maximum results in a minimum amount of time—if you fall back into old habits, however, these techniques and the overall program will lose the desired effect.

Still, exceptions can be made. You'll learn that the bulk of your eating (pun intended) should take place between 10 a.m. and 2 p.m. If you have a business dinner to attend, or a special meal with friends and family, enjoy your experience and make adjustments the following day. If you're new to the program and crave sugar as I do, by all means you can sometimes have your "cake and eat it too." Just do it between 10 a.m. and 2 p.m. when the digestive fire is highest.

By the second week, you will find desserts will begin to lose their allure. Additionally, if a specific herb or spice does not agree with your taste, then skip it. If the exercises suggested don't feel right or take too long, make adjustments. If in moments of stress you don't always breathe from your diaphragm, go on breathing anyway!

The *Radiance Program* is designed for all women, although men can benefit as well. I recognize that each of us is unique. What works for one—due to circumstances, body characteristics, schedule, mindset, lifestyle, and so on—will not work as well for another. Therefore, fine tune to your needs.

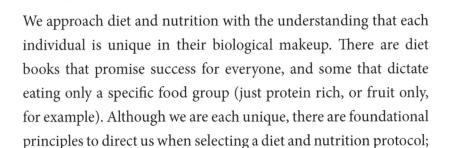

We approach diet and nutrition with the understanding that each individual is unique in their biological makeup. There are diet books that promise success for everyone, and some that dictate eating only a specific food group (just protein rich, or fruit only, for example). Although we are each unique, there are foundational principles to direct us when selecting a diet and nutrition protocol; *Return to Radiance* provides these guidelines.

When we turn to exercise, I believe your own body should dictate what exercises you perform, so long as you get *enough* movement in your day to keep your mind and body metabolism in balance. The exercises in this program are specifically chosen to build your metabolic fire, the foundation for energy and rejuvenation. In addition, I emphasize the importance of diaphragmatic breathing so that it becomes natural to you, as this is the link that connects the mind and the body.

Because we know the energy of the mind is the essence of life, there is a skillset for you to establish practice. Meditation is the tool to make this happen.

The program works from the ground up, building our foundation to collect and contain our essential energy so that we can have access to working with concentration.

# HIGHLIGHTS

Radiance only *seems* mysterious. You can solve the mystery when there is mastery of the energy in your body, breath and mind. Mastery starts with awareness followed by creating skillful habits.

This overall program is more important than its specifics, but if you follow it, you will see results. As you start, remember:

- Overeating or eating the wrong foods is like putting wet wood on a fire. Metabolic fire is what gives us radiance—the luminous vitality that dwells within us.

- Eating processed, stale, pesticide-laden, or canned foods is like using low-test gasoline when your car requires premium.

- When cells age or become damaged, raw fruits and vegetables—the best source of vitamins and minerals—will replenish them.

- The best healer of the body is the mind, and the mind and body are one.

- Caffeine, diet pills, and extended fasting are sure ways to destroy vitality. All will reduce or eliminate the production of essential enzymes and hormones, and while you may lose weight temporarily, you'll also be losing your foundation. Your body will be feeding on itself to get the nourishment that it seeks.

- Diaphragmatic breathing is the most efficient way to breathe, as it vitalizes cellular mechanisms.

- Stress adversely affects our essential hormones; proper breathing practices reduce stress.

- Exercise can cause problems if it creates stress rather than energy flow.
- Both the upper and lower body should be exercised, since both areas affect the overall stability of your body.
- Metabolic regulation is most accessible when working with the abdominal and sacral region of the body.
- Your own radiance will evoke the radiance in others, women as well as men.
- The best of all vitalizing substances is the recognition of who you are. The best way to find the truest expression of you is to go inward toward the deepest part of self. When you discover your authentic being, then you have returned to radiance.

Before you start the program, put a check mark beside each symptom or action that applies to you.

☐ Fatigue or chronic tiredness
☐ Digestive Problems
☐ Constipation
☐ Diarrhea
☐ Bladder problems
☐ Menstrual problems
☐ Hormonal imbalance
☐ Lack of exercise
☐ Stiffness
☐ Inflammation
☐ Overweight
☐ Underweight
☐ Breathe from chest
☐ Frequent sickness
☐ Extreme emotional fluctuations
☐ Feel emotionally burdened
☐ Depression
☐ Anxiety
☐ Lack of creativity
☐ Irritability

- ☐ Low self-esteem
- ☐ Feel overworked
- ☐ Difficulty getting up in the morning
- ☐ Insomnia

- ☐ Feel hesitant
- ☐ Feel unattractive
- ☐ Feel shy
- ☐ Feel fear
- ☐ Feel unloved

If you've checked a number of these—or even one—read on!

# CHAPTER 2

———O———

# Energy Modulation

*Anyone who has seen a newborn baby realizes that vibrant energy is with us when we are born. Later in life, it is up to us to regulate our energy reserves, paying attention to collecting, containing, and concentrating it for times of need.*

To be radiant is to be vital. To be vital requires that we are able to have the energy to carry out what we want to do in a stable and comfortable way.

Energy on all levels—physical, emotional, psychological, and spiritual—is acquired through the foods we eat, the way we breathe, and our thought processes. The vibrations that pulse through our body and mind from the food we eat, as well as from the thoughts that we feed our mind, influence the nourishment and health of our mind and body. Most people think that they can get energy from a supercharged beverage. You will surely have an energy jolt and function on high speed—for a little while. When you find yourself winding down, your energy will be dissipated, and often your mood becomes glum. The beverage utilizes the energy reserves in your body and spends them, leaving the brain fatigued and the mind scattered, and your system craves more.

It is possible, however, to be energetic without using up your reserves; indeed, you'll be replenishing them. Instead of consuming a supercharged beverage first thing in the morning, I often suggest clients drink warm water with lemon or make a fresh vegetable juice smoothie. The smoothie most will likely satisfy your brain's need for food and provide an uplift, while nourishing your brain with the necessary nutrients for energy and focus. If they choose to have coffee or tea, I offer it as an option later in the morning around 10 a.m. To slow down the "sudden jolt" of caffeine, I suggest they add a little fat to their coffee or tea, like coconut oil or ghee.

―――――○―――――

## Your Energy Is Contingent Upon What You Eat

Sophie, thirty-five, is slightly overweight, and is looking to lose about ten pounds. What's more, she feels tired, with little or no focus, as she complains about fatigue. Exercise that she once loved now feels like a chore, and rather than go to the gym after work, she prefers to go home and snack as she connects with her friends on social media. It becomes obvious through our discussion that she's come to see me in hopes of a quick fix.

"Tell me about your diet, Sophie."

"I eat well," she tells me sincerely. "A wholesome breakfast, no more than a salad and yogurt for lunch, meat, chicken, or fish for dinner, lots of vegetables, and plenty of daily snacks but certainly no late-night snacks."

"Bread?"

"When I go to a restaurant, I'll have a slice or two before the meal comes. And of course there's toast with my eggs in the morning."

"Desserts?"

"Plenty of fruit," she says defensively. Then, blushing, "And some ice cream for dinner. I can't resist it. But never more than two scoops." She becomes defensive again. "My doctor tells me it's a balanced diet."

In a way, it is. It's not the food intake that's the problem, it's *when* she eats what she eats.

I think of my friend Nancy, one of the most vibrant and radiant people that I know, age fifty-five. She and I have discussed diet many times, and I know that she, too, likes her sweets, chicken, fish, and bread. Indeed, Nancy's caloric intake is as high as Sophie's, even at her age, and she eats her "comfort foods." Nancy has roasted whole oats, fruit, and fresh juice for breakfast, at lunch, she eats vegetables and rice; occasionally, she eats fish or lean chicken dishes at night. She avoids bread and desserts after 2 p.m.

Nancy's eating is in tune with her metabolic clock. She doesn't eat a big breakfast because her metabolism is sluggish in the morning—after all, it's been "asleep" for seven or eight hours and needs time to fire up. She eats her main meal at lunch. Looking at nature, the sun is highest between 10 a.m. and 2 p.m.; likewise, our body temperature is also higher than at other times of day. Food ingested during this time period provides the most nourishment for creating and sustaining vitality. Additionally, when night time comes, Nancy will have given her body ample time for digestion; her dinner, eaten before 7 p.m., will not burden it. She is making sure that her food intake is energy-efficient for her brain. She does not gain weight, she exudes vitality, and her mind is focused; she is happy and healthy.

For Sophie, I recommend a few adjustments. Two meals a day are all she needs, though she can have fruit and fresh fruit juice for breakfast. I advise her to substitute rice for her bread since she is gluten sensitive, and if she needs desserts, eat them once per week. Most importantly, I advise Sophie that on "dessert" day it would be best for her if she eats it early, so she has ample time to digest and reset her metabolism. Otherwise, she can have some protein at lunch and avoid the brain sluggishness at the end of the day.

If you place too much burden on the digestive system by eating big meals at night or by grazing throughout the day, then the brain and body cannot perform their "house cleaning" duties. In the end, the system will not function properly. At the very least, your energy level will go down, while at the worst you may develop allergies, immune-resistant issues, and even weight gain. Additionally, you may experience a loss of mental focus and agility.

The brain is continuously in an active metabolic state and does not have fuel storage like our muscles or liver; it requires a greater supply of nutrients and prefers a slow and steady release. Additionally, the brain cleanses and detoxes itself during restful sleep,[1] so it is important not to eat late in the evening because it interferes with these "house cleaning" processes.

Complex carbohydrates, those found in grains, fruits, vegetables, and legumes, are slow-and-steady types. You can find them in whole, natural foods and are "slow and steady" because they take longer to digest; they are composed of long chains of sugar molecules surrounded by cellulose fiber that resists digestion. This is a bit like the way a time-release vitamin capsule works. The liver, as well as the digestive system, gradually breaks these long chains down into shorter glucose molecules to be released between meals and fuel the brain.

Carbohydrates that come from refined sugar—cakes, pastries, and other white flour products—on the other hand, are easy to digest and lack this natural-delay mechanism. Therefore, the sugar is released into the bloodstream quickly and is exhausted just as quickly, leaving the brain fatigued.

There are many people advocating the keto diet right now. Although I am not a proponent of this, there does seem to be some benefit in the short term. Keep in mind, carbohydrates in the form of whole grains are superior for your colon health. These complex carbohydrates are also favorable for your gut microbiome, those colonies of bacteria that keep your immunity strong and your moods happy when properly fed the correct foods.

## METABOLIC REGULATION

Anyone who has seen a newborn baby realizes that vibrant energy is our birthright. Later in life, it is up to us to regulate our energy reserves, paying attention to collecting, containing, and concentrating it for times of need. We used to believe that by the time we are forty, we have "spent" more than half of our energy reserves and that by the age of sixty-five, we have fully depleted them. Now we know that such ideas are not necessarily accurate; a woman in her sixties or seventies can be just as vital as a woman in her twenties. This is not implying that we don't age, but suggests that we can regulate our reserves by adopting a "yogi" lifestyle—one which creates habits that collect, contain, and concentrate energy.

If we wish to remain youthful and radiant, we must be mindful and replenish our energy reserves, eat well, exercise intelligently, breathe diaphragmatically, and meditate regularly. The trick is to build from the foundation up. If throughout our lifetime we do not nourish our body and mind, our vitality will dissipate at an increasing rate. When this happens, we will have a difficult time bringing our organism back into balance, in other words, to heal. If, however, we fine-tune our mind and nourish our body, that will lead to longevity. If we can grasp the concept that maintenance equals vitality, then optimal health and radiance will be ours at any age.

Energy is a primordial force that permeates all living things. It is invisible, yet if we stop to experience it—to "see" it—this force is as palpable as wind or fire. We call it the life force. In Yoga Science it is called *prana*, and in Chinese Medicine, *chi*. This life force moves through and sustains all matter in the universe, and is recognized by all the world's cultures. It is needed to build and maintain cell structures, to move, to reproduce, to think, to feel. Without it, there is no joy, no love, no radiance, no life.

Western medical science says that energy comes from matter, namely food. Eastern science adds the subtle aspects of breath to the equation. As mammals, we obtain energy from the combustion of foods containing carbohydrates, proteins, and fats, combined with oxygen. Some of the fuel is burned immediately to give us instant energy, while some is stored in various parts of the body to be released as energy during times of need—for example between meals.

Metabolism comprises all the biological and chemical reactions that are required to carry on life's processes, from the manufacturing of hormones to the building of bones, from breathing to moving, to being radiant. Each of our 100 billion neurons that transmit nerve signals at up to 200 mph requires energy to function. These neurons are the cells responsible for cellular communication that send and receive electro-chemical signals to and from the brain and nervous system. Each cell has within it these "powerhouses" called mitochondria. Within the mitochondria, cellular respiration occurs. This process produces energy by combining carbon atoms with oxygen in what is known as the citric acid cycle (or the TCA cycle). The citric acid cycle gets its products from molecules that have been metabolized in our brain and other organs of our body. Glucose molecules, stemming from the breakdown of carbohydrates (sugars), feed into the TCA cycle to support the energy systems that extend throughout the body. Fatty acid molecules, resulting from the breakdown of fat, also feed into it and help to build the structure of the central nervous system, specifically the brain. The power derived from these molecules drives the processes of the brain so that there is energy for transmission of impulses, as well as synaptic plasticity—the ability of the brain to grow new pathways—a process required for learning and memory.

It appears then that mitochondria play a key role in the brain and the normal functioning of our cells. Mitochondrial cells—energy-producing cells—may become damaged or compromised, as a result of poor dietary and lifestyle habits. Mitochondrial dysfunction has been linked to neurodegenerative diseases that lead to impaired cognitive ability (such as Alzheimer's or Parkinson's).[2,3] This explains the need for a moderate-fat diet, diaphragmatic breathing, systematic relaxation, and meditation.

## NUTRITION AND ENERGY MODULATION

You are what you eat, or rather, what you digest. Digestion is the assimilation and utilization of nutrients, and the elimination of by-products. Food is transformed into energy when it is broken down into molecules that can be used by our cells.

Proper digestion depends on three components: the *timing* of when we eat, the *quantity* of what we eat, and the *quality* of what we eat. To understand why all three are vital, it's important to know something about the digestive process.

Digestion begins when food first enters the mouth, where it is carefully and rigorously chewed. Chewing is an essential part of promoting good digestion (it's surprising how many people simply swallow their food as if they were equipped with a gizzard.) Chewing *well* not only allows you to taste and enjoy your food (which cuts down on overeating), it also stimulates specific brain centers. Additionally, the process mixes the food with saliva. Saliva contains a substance, Immunoglobulin A (IgA), that protects the upper digestive tract from bacteria found in food. Though sometimes, the bacteria are heavily concentrated or your system is so weak that you develop stomach issues, or other conditions, despite the protection.

From the mouth, food travels to the stomach by way of the esophagus. Once it has arrived in the stomach, it is further broken down. Here, from one to two quarts of digestive juices are produced per day, the main one being hydrochloric acid. In the stomach, protein is digested, minerals are separated from the food, and bacteria that escaped the saliva are re-attached. The food, now transformed to chyme, proceeds to the small intestine, where most of the digestion and assimilation of nutrients takes place. At this point, the chyme mixes with alkaline enzymes to increase its absorption.

The bulk of the matter then proceeds to the large intestine, where it is worked on by microbes (microflora), and the waste products are eliminated. Some microbes promote health; others are toxic and cause disease. Microbes play an essential role in metabolizing nutrients, vitamins, drugs, hormones, and disease-causing agents. The integrity of the intestinal tract's microflora (microbiome) determines the health and vitality of your brain and overall wellness. When we overeat, drink too much, or encounter stress, we add to the burden of the digestive system. Like a car running on inferior oil or not tuned properly, our body-mind complex cannot run at peak efficiency.

How many of us have an efficient digestive system? Not many. We may have distended stomachs, or complaints of heartburn, indigestion, and constipation. Just about everyone experiences digestive problems on occasion. They're some of the most common complaints in doctors' offices. For more than 10 million people, gas, bloating, constipation, diarrhea, or heartburn are a regular occurrence.[4] When we don't absorb the proper nutrients, we get tired, irritable, tense. Our brain function becomes foggy, fatigued, and downright dull. Imagine overeating cookies or candies. Not only will you stop tasting them, but your digestive system will be hard-pressed to break down the components.

When I meet clients, the top item on the agenda is to improve their digestion. Even those who come to me to learn meditation find it surprising that I adjust their diet first. Why? Digestive disturbance leads to a disturbed mind. Once we accomplish eating to insure more balance, 90% of digestive symptoms "mysteriously" disappear and our mood improves.

After I began a special diet that eliminated cold foods, sugar, and most dairy products, my energy improved immeasurably. I had been eating too much bread and too many starches as a matter of convenience and my body wasn't able to digest them fast enough.

I felt exhausted all the time due to the inflammation that was occurring. When I cut down on the simple starches, eliminated wheat products from the USA, and incorporated easily digested foods like beans and rice, I felt much more vital and focused. I will speak more on this in a later chapter.

Let's come back now to the three components of proper digestion: timing, quality, and quantity. I'll take them one at a time.

## Timing

The Chinese system of medicine holds that energy, or *chi*, flows through meridians or energy channels in a specific pattern. Every two hours, a different organ dominates the flow of *chi* in the body. The small intestine, it is noted, dominates from 1 p.m. to 3 p.m. Since it is the organ primarily responsible for digestion and absorption, 1 p.m. to 3 p.m. is the best time for food to be assimilated. From 5 a.m. to 7 a.m., on the other hand, the large intestine dominates. Since it is here that toxic waste is stored, it makes sense that early morning is the most appropriate time to eliminate.

In the Ayurvedic system of medicine—the science of health and longevity—a twenty-four-hour cycle is divided into six segments, instead of twelve, but the principle is essentially the same. If we follow the energy patterns during the day with respect to our bodily functions, then our brain will maintain balance and allow energy to flow freely. For example, in the mornings between 6 a.m. and 10 a.m., we feel most energetic or fresh; what we eat during this time should be cleansing and light so as not to impede that energy. (Test yourself. Many people may feel that they need food as soon as they get up. Train yourself to eat a piece of fruit and notice how good the food tastes in the next phase of the cycle!)

From 10 a.m. to 2 p.m., our metabolic energy is at its highest. Digestive enzymes are up-regulated (activated) and food burns most efficiently. During this time of day you can eat anything you want, but be careful not to eat too much; you do not want to smother your digestive fire.

During the last cycle, from 2 p.m. to 6 p.m., we feel active and light, in some cases even light-headed. Here, we tend to go for sugar and other stimulating foods because we need a boost at the end of the day. Far better to choose food that is stabilizing and moist- meaning foods that are complex like whole grains that regulate blood sugar levels, and "moist" referring to those foods you do not need to wash down with water. Choose fresh fruit over dry fruit, cooked vegetables over raw, baked potatoes over potato chips, oatmeal over sugary cereal, whole-grain bread over white bread. Eat soups and protein-rich foods, but avoid stimulating foods containing caffeine or sugar—e.g., coffee and dessert.

The energy cycle repeats itself through the next twelve hours, but instead of consuming the food intake of the day, don't eat anything at all. (Plain water or water with lemon is the exception.) The reason for doing this is that our digestive system needs rest for at least twelve hours daily, and an overnight "fast" is the way to make sure this is accomplished. More about the overnight fast later.

From a physiological viewpoint, the period from dinner to breakfast is the best time for the body to do its major house cleaning. If you think of the intervals between daytime meals as times for dusting, then nighttime is for sweeping. Not eating before going to sleep allows the metabolic processes to work most efficiently. If, for whatever reason, you must have something before bedtime, try taking just a glass of water, or water with lemon; if the water does not satisfy you then have some herbal tea (without caffeine), and lastly, milk that has been boiled for three minutes to aid digestion. The nighttime "fast" enables us to process undigested food left from the day, restore cellular function, and repair any damage to the digestive system.

From the above, it's easy to see that the best time for our brains to recharge is in-between meals and especially at night. Our energy and flexibility are highest in the morning and early evening when our stomachs are not overloaded, and our vitality flows. Americans, though, are a nation of grazers. We pay little to no attention to our metabolic clock. Since we eat throughout the day, we give little thought to the best time for food or rest. It is a pity. Try eating the way I recommend and your brain health will improve, I assure you. Eat at the right time, rest, exercise your body, and your vitality will increase.

## Quality

A nourished body and balanced mind is the foundation of radiance. Our vitality depends on the energy that we derive from the food we eat, and the quality of that food determines how our body's reserves will be restored or depleted.

Since 1916, the Department of Agriculture has recommended what food groups are necessary for an adequate diet. In 1992, food groups were officially organized into a "food guide pyramid," with bread, cereal, rice, and pasta at the bottom; fruits, vegetables, meats, dairy products in the middle; and fats, oils, and sweets at the top. The pyramid is meant as a guide for what we should eat each day and in what quantities in order to maintain a balanced diet (i.e., including more of those foods at the bottom and less of those at the top).

In 2011, the USDA issued new, long-overdue dietary guidelines that replaced the food pyramid with the "MyPlate Model," comprising four sections: grains, vegetables, fruits, and proteins, accompanied by dairy.[5] However, because agricultural-governmental interests may slightly distort the model, we should look beyond what the government advises. We need to consider what a vital energy food-plate model would look like for our unique bio-psychological matrix.

The *Radiance Diet* is somewhat different, in that it substitutes beans for most animal-derived protein, limits dairy consumption to organic and not necessarily low fat, and emphasizes fresh food and whole grains. Additionally, this diet eliminates or minimizes white-flour products and genetically-modified products, with GMO wheat being at the top of the list.

The components of food may be classified as micronutrients (vitamins, minerals, and phytochemicals) and macronutrients (carbohydrates, proteins, and fats) with micronutrients playing a vital role in the metabolism of the macronutrients. As we know, though, food is more complex than its physical components, it has an essence—life force—just as we do. Our food eventually becomes our consciousness. It is, therefore, necessary to choose foods that support and nourish a clear, calm, and tranquil mind— a radiant mind.

Let's suppose that the food you eat has been concentrated through the process of dehydration and preserved with chemicals to prolong its shelf-life (though, not its life force). You will still be eating carbohydrates, proteins, and fats, and if you take vitamin supplements, and according to Western theory, you will be "satisfying" your body's basic needs. You'll be getting the right molecules, but as Eastern science has pointed out, and many

Western nutritional biochemists agree, it won't be giving you the energy you need. You'll feel heavy and dull—devitalized. If you keep eating this way for a long time, you'll feel older than your years. There will be nothing in your system to restore your vital energy that supports your brain and your entire body's functions.

I am not in favor of microwaving either, although, most nutritionists would disagree. When you use a microwave the taste of food is altered, and this is an indication of molecular change. Who knows what effect microwaves have on the biological level and the assimilation process, not to mention your consciousness? I suspect that it will change the way food gets incorporated into the cells. The result—deficient vitality. My advice to my clients who feel brain fatigue and fogginess is to stick to preparing fresh foods daily, or at least every few days.

Suzanne, a client of mine, was one of those women who could not live without her microwave. It's possible she had not used a conventional oven in the last ten years. If she cooked, she used a microwave, but she did not cook often. She had a diet shake for breakfast, diet cuisine for lunch, and a salad mix for dinner. Suzanne was a thin woman, so weight was not a prevailing issue for her. She was concerned about why she felt spacey and ungrounded. When looking at her diet, I could see that Suzanne was not consuming enough moist, fresh food; as a result, her essence was a bit dry. Her skin became dull and lacked luster. Her radiance was just not there. To change things, she would have to start nourishing herself with fresh food and balanced meals.

It's easy to see for yourself that eating fresh food makes a difference. Try this experiment: for a week, eat only pre-prepared foods. Then for another week, eat only fresh food. Take note of your energy, the ability to focus, and your overall emotional state during each week. I promise there will be a huge difference; you will not go back to processed foods again. If this exercise seems too difficult, prepare and drink some fresh orange juice, and then try juice from a can, container or bottle. See how you feel. It's a very informative exercise.

If we equate the energy of food with voltage, processed food gives off 100 volts of energy or less, and fresh food gives off the equivalent of 200 volts of energy. However, eating fresh foods alone isn't enough. The answer lies within our soil, systematically being demineralized and its microbiome destroyed. Pollutants fill our air and water. Even when we eat fresh food, we may not meet the minimum requirements of basic nutrients or important trace minerals like selenium and zinc.

Later I'll be recommending supplements such as phytonutrients, herbs, vitamins, and minerals to help complete your diet. These, however, are not an equal substitute for quality fresh foods. For now, I want to stress the importance of the fuel that regulates your energy and vitality. Devitalized food and inadequate amounts of trace minerals and vitamins leave the average person energy-deficient; this can result in anxiety, depression, memory issues, and lack of vitality. When you're young, you have a natural resilience that cannot be completely lost by an improper diet. As you age, however, this is no longer the case. You will begin to see how all of your functions are linked to your dietary practices and consequently, to your thinking patterns. We will cover thinking patterns in a later chapter.

By correcting your diet, you can do wonders for your overall brain health and cognitive capacity, even after years of consuming processed and canned foods. If the only thing this book accomplishes is to convince you to eat better, it will have achieved a great deal of its purpose.

## Quantity

○ How many times have you told yourself to stop eating, that you don't need anymore?

○ How easy is it to get up in the morning after a late night meal?

○ How long did it take for you to realize that eating a full meal before a mental task inhibits your ability to focus and concentrate?

Obvious questions with obvious answers point to one conclusion; excess food consumption causes loss of vitality, dulls our awareness, blunts our alertness, and produces fatigue. Have you ever felt vital after consuming a four-course meal? Eating that much food makes it hard to just get up from the table!

We all know that eating extra food doesn't translate into additional nutrients, but sometimes we still overeat. That fifth bite of chocolate cake tastes no different from the first, yet we still shovel it into our mouths. In reality, we tend to overeat the foods that aren't nourishing. Our mind and palette find these foods satisfying at first, yet in a short time we feel unsatisfied. Paradoxically we crave more.

We mistakenly believe that if we keep eating, eventually we will be satisfied. Overeating puts a strain on our digestive system (which can't accommodate the food we consumed), it also places stress on our brain, nervous system, and our consciousness. It is far more difficult for us to operate on any level—physical, emotional, intellectual, spiritual—if our body is struggling to digest the food it has just taken in.

I don't recommend under-eating either; it leads to a decrease in optimal function. By under-eating, I mean not taking in enough nutrients to support a highly-functional brain and a calm, focused mind. This is not the same as cutting down on calories, where caloric restriction can increase life span. When we skip meals, drink diet soda and coffee in between meals to curb appetite, and allow those substances to take the place of meals, it leads to nutrient depletion. When we starve our brains regularly in an attempt to stay thin, we are actually putting incredible stress on our system. Random, intermittent fasting is included in this analysis. Indeed, over-dieting by skipping meals is one of the most hazardous threats to our overall vitality. What we must strive for is balance—a tuning of the brain and mind to become consciously aware of the process to feel vital and alive. This book serves as that guide for operating at full capacity, for playing, for thinking, for feeling, for living.

## BREATHING FOR MAXIMUM ENERGY

The way we breathe is not particularly associated with health (unless you stopped doing it—then you would be deceased). Thanks to our growing awareness of Yoga Science, we know just how essential proper breathing is to good health.

Very few people associate breathing with energy. For the average person, breathing is patently the mechanical means for moving air in and out of the lungs so we can replenish our red blood cells with oxygen. However, Eastern science—more specifically Swara yoga— has added another dimension to the breathing process—*prana*, the life force, our subtle energy.

Breathing is the bridge between ourselves and the earth's energetic rhythm. Our brain's vitality depends largely on our ability to absorb this subtle energy. While this may sound mystical or New Age, there is a scientific basis for it.

To understand breathing as it relates to energy, we must look at the autonomic nervous system. The autonomic nervous system is divided into two branches: the **parasympathetic**, which controls the slowing of the heart rate, the regulation of digestion, and the clearing of toxins from the body; and the **sympathetic**, which controls our arousal mechanisms and prepares us to take action. The latter comes into play when we are forced into sudden action or experience sudden stress. For example, if we perceive that we are in danger, the sympathetic nervous system will speed up our heart rate, shoot adrenaline into our bloodstream, cause our palms to sweat, and force us into the instantaneous decision of whether to fight, flee or freeze. Both the parasympathetic and sympathetic systems are affected by the motion of our lungs. When we breathe from the chest, we activate the sympathetic system, but when we breathe from the diaphragm, we balance both systems. Thus the functioning of the autonomic nervous system is directly linked to breathing. When we breathe in, the sympathetic tone increases; when we breathe out, the parasympathetic tone enables us to slow down and increase control.

Breathing is a function so automatic that we don't recognize that there are in fact "good" and "not so good" ways to breathe; the way we breathe directly relates to our energy and our brain's vitality. We breathe in and out, anywhere from 23,000 to 26,000 times per day or roughly 15-18 times per minute. This may be considered normal, but it is not the most healthy. In contrast, if we breathe diaphragmatically, the rate is 9,000 to 13,000 times per day or 6-12 times per minute.[6] This is optimal.

Breathing goes on whether or not you pay attention to it. When you are fully aware of your breath, you can gain control over your autonomic nervous system. When you learn to bring the breath under your conscious control, you can use it to regulate your vital functions, including your metabolism.

I'll go much deeper into the physiological aspects of breath later. For now, to help you become aware that there are different ways to breathe, try the following simple experiment.

Lie on your back and relax. Let the floor support your weight. Gently place one of your hands over your navel. Breathe in as you normally would. As you begin to inhale, do you notice your abdomen expand like a balloon? Don't force your belly; notice how it moves. Exhale. Your abdomen should deflate. Did it? If so, you are already 75% further along toward nourishing your brain.

**Benefits of Diaphragmatic Breathing**
*   You have cut down on the number of breaths per minute, increasing respiratory efficiency.
*   You have saved strain on your heart (rapid breaths lead to increased heart rate).
*   You have conserved energy.
*   You have given a powerful propellant to your blood circulation, sending more oxygen to the brain.
*   You have greatly enhanced your lung capacity. For every extra millimeter your diaphragm stretches during inhalation, your lung capacity increases by a volume of 250 – 300 milliliters.
*   You have massaged the glands and organs in the abdominal cavity, particularly the adrenals located above the kidneys. These are directly responsible for the manufacturing of hormones that benefit the brain.
*   You have brought your mind under your conscious control.

This book will teach you the technique for diaphragmatic breathing, which I sometimes call metabolic breathing because it enhances your overall metabolism. It is simple, natural, and the way you were born to breathe. It is revitalizing, and it opens the door for you to experience your inner radiance. It just takes a little practice.

## EXERCISES FOR VITAL ENERGY

Olivia, an actress and singer, knew how to breathe diaphragmatically; she had been trained to do so by way of her singing career. Her diet was good too, with the exception of her monthly binging tied to her hormonal fluctuations. Her binges caused emotional issues—irritability and anger. She came to see me about her feelings of fatigue, emotional instability, and sluggishness. Olivia's weight was on the rise, a factor that could have proven detrimental to her career. I noticed that she lacked overall muscle tone except in the area around her rib cage, which she had developed through diaphragmatic breathing. I suggested an exercise program that focused on her abdominal area, followed by a ten-minute systematic relaxation exercise. After three weeks, Olivia reported that she had more energy and confidence. She was an accomplished woman, yet her story emphasized to me how essential exercise and relaxation are to living a balanced and vital life.

No matter what type of exercise you do, you will improve your blood circulation, bring nutrition to your cells and glands, rejuvenate the function of tissues, and aid in the proper elimination of waste. The best exercises are aligned with breathing and relaxation, a gold standard.

When you don't exercise, you're susceptible to hypertension, sluggish circulation, and poor cardiac output; this leads to shortness of breath and the risk of heart attacks, erosion of muscle tone, and so many other vulnerabilities.

In order to exercise, you need oxygen and glycogen. Breathing supplies the oxygen; eating supplies the carbohydrates necessary to make glycogen. That's one of the reasons all three are inextricably linked.

Exercise is important for the strengthening of our muscles which contain mitochondria. These are responsible for cellular respiration. The mitochondria generate ATP, a high-energy molecule used by all living cells to transfer chemical energy. The more muscle we develop from exercising, the more mitochondria we create to meet our need for energy. Muscle development also keeps our weight down, improves posture and mood, balances hormones, and increases circulation. If we then coordinate this with proper breathing, the benefits are profound. Keep in mind, though, that muscles, like every other part of the body, can become overworked. We don't want to cause them stress; we want them to be stable and comfortable.

Most of us become stiffer as we age. The area surrounded by our hips, where our sexual organs are housed, becomes frozen and locked. When we work with movements that free up the sacral region, tension is released, and energy begins to flow freely. As a result, our foundation in movement becomes strong, stable, and we rejuvenate.

According to Ayurvedic and Traditional Chinese Medicine (TCM), metabolic energy manifests itself in the process of digestion at the solar plexus region. If we activate this area, we will increase our metabolic power. In conjunction with the exercises for the lower abdomen, along with proper breathing and a balanced diet, we activate the solar plexus area—our *hara*—and our vitality increases. Then we can begin to experience our inner radiance.

Vast differences do exist between different exercise programs.

As you'll see in the *Return to Radiance* program, my recommendations take into consideration both physiological and psychological processes, rather than being confined to physical movement alone. This program will serve to develop a strong and stable physical presence, as well as a body consciousness. In time, when you experience the freedom of movement through these sequences, your body will release the stored emotions.

Before you begin any program, determine the state of your health and establish your goals. Working with weights, for example, encourages the growth of lean muscle tissue and bone strength, some of which can be lost through dieting (another reason why dieting and exercise work well together). Aerobic exercise is good for the heart and overall circulation. Yoga exercise, namely asana, when done skillfully and not just as a form of calisthenics, can serve to collect, concentrate, and circulate your vital energy resulting in total transformation. The primary goal is to enhance your life span and metabolic efficiency of your body and mind—and by doing so, your radiance.

When you begin exercising, evaluate your appetite and mood, and record your experience. If you become ravenous within one to two hours after working out, cut down on your activity; you don't want to eat so much in compensation for exercising that the result is actually weight gain.

If, after two hours, or even the next day, the idea of another session of exercise seems burdensome, you probably did too much in the first place. A balanced program will leave you feeling refreshed and complete. If you feel out of balance, adjust by consulting a qualified person, or change the length and the variety of your routine. You are the best person to regulate what feels right to you.

I am often asked what is the best time to do yoga, eat, meditate, or just do general exercise. I would say it depends on your particular lifestyle and your goals. If you are a "morning person," then exercise may be best in the morning; however, if you tend to be more alert in the evening, do it at night. Generally, if there is some resistance to a lifestyle habit change, it is best to do it in the morning. This will provide your mind with a positive habit to support you the rest of the day. You will not have to think about it. If you need the morning to use your alert mind for writing, meditating or some other activity, then choose the evening for exercise. Morning exercisers might want to consider eating a wholesome breakfast afterward to keep the body and mind well-nourished. Afternoons tend to be the worst time to exercise unless you are committed to a structured class. The reason for this is because blood sugar tends to plummet around 4 p.m., and you may feel a bit tired. It will require more willpower to participate. Exercising in the evenings will rekindle your energy, but it is also when you tend to be most tired. If you have a goal to lose weight, then evening exercise works; however, the downside is it may be more difficult for you to relax and sleep. It's up to you. The keys to your exercise program are consistency and discipline.

Try any program for at least three weeks, this is the least amount of time needed to sense changes in your body. This is not to say that you won't feel changes sooner, but it takes time to change the physical body when you are working from the inside out. The programs that I create for students and clients working directly with me require that they follow the routine for a full forty days. Their programs are carefully structured for their specific issues and goals. For our purposes here, try the program for three weeks and if it feels great to you, continue for another two weeks before going to the next level. Make sure you exercise four or five times a week. Less than that and your metabolism won't change. Research has shown that people who exercise four or five times per week keep their arteries younger and stronger.[7]

> **Note:** If you practice "yoga postures," you can do them everyday. The physical exercises I am referring to are weight-bearing exercises and aerobics. Again, consistency and discipline are key. The more you bring exercise into your life, the easier and more natural it becomes. Its effects are transforming!

You'll find a complete three-week starter program for diet, breathing, and exercise at the end of this book that incorporates all of the above. You may, however, need a bit more convincing before you make a commitment to it.

I want to talk a little about biochemistry. Don't be put off. It's simple material, and knowledge of it can feed your mind and add radiance to your life. Remember knowledge and experience go hand-in-hand. You need the knowledge to engage the limbic brain (the place that sustains our best intentions) and experience to digest and utilize that knowledge.

# CHAPTER 3

————————◯————————

# The Biochemistry of Wellness

*The deep state of rest changes the neurochemical transmission in our brain. Each of these naturally-occurring brain chemicals has been linked to different aspects of how we feel.*

Ours is a strange society. We're most likely concerned about health only when we are fearful that we are losing our youth, usually when it is too late and we're sick. Currently we have many doctors to treat symptoms, but few to prevent or even cure illness. We think that our body will just break down as we get older, that frailty is a"natural" part of aging, and it's "okay" that our vitality and enthusiasm diminishes and our passion for life wanes as time goes by.

I think of myself as a teacher and practitioner of wellness. Women contact me about health-related issues from concerns like eating too much, loss of stamina, feeling sad or anxious, lack of focus, and so on, to more chronic conditions such as stress-related body stiffness, menstrual-emotional issues, digestive disturbances, and negative thinking. I find that outward focused activities consume most of their time during the day. They do not consider doing something for their health and wellbeing until it gets to the point where more days are unhappy than happy. However, after we work together, these women leave with a renewed interest in wellbeing, and their feminine essence is enhanced. I am convinced that the program presented in this book will be just as helpful for you. It is to be undertaken *before* your boat reaches the waterfall and is about to plummet over the edge; in other words, before you get sick. So begin now to follow a plan that will help keep you radiant far longer than you thought possible.

Our physical vitality lies in biochemistry—the science of the composition, structure, properties, and reaction of matter—as it affects our biological processes. These processes constitute our metabolism. I am going to show you how your diet, movement, breathing patterns, and thinking (mental state) are connected to your metabolism. Establishing skillful habits in these areas supports your health and well being.

—————O—————

According to Western science, humans have five vital organs that are essential for survival. These are the brain, heart, kidneys, lungs, and liver. In Traditional Chinese Medicine (TCM), the heart, liver, spleen, lung, kidney, gallbladder, stomach, small intestine, large intestine, bladder, and triple-warmer are used in medical diagnostic protocols.

## Brain

The brain makes it possible for us to think, feel, remember, and operate in both the external and internal world. In Western medicine, the brain is not viewed the same way as it is in TCM. Modern medicine views the brain as the most important organ, acting as the body's command center, receiving and sending signals to other organs. In brain disease, the focus is on treating the brain separately from the rest of the body. In Traditional Chinese Medicine, brain diseases are regarded as systemic diseases rather than disorders of a single organ (i.e., the brain). Therefore, TCM treats brain disease by normalizing and balancing the functional activity and interaction of the liver, heart, spleen, kidney and lung.[1] Western medicine now recognizes the bidirectional communication between the brain and the gut; Eastern medicine built its foundation on this vital connection. *Feeling Good Matters, The Yoga of Mind, Medicine and Healing*[2] elaborates on the science of gut health, and the Radiance Program has this as a cornerstone.

## Heart

The human heart regulates the body. It is responsible for an even and regular pulse, so that our circulation works efficiently. As the heart pumps blood throughout our body, our brain and organ systems are nourished. It has a direct influence on our vitality and spirit. Many mindfulness and meditation programs suggest that we open our hearts to experience love and compassion. However, we cannot do this easily unless we address our ability to focus our mind. Our heart center opens spontaneously when we strengthen our other centers through nourishing and cleansing practices.

The Vedic Sciences of Ayurveda, Yoga, and Tantra all view the heart as an important energetic center in the body, a hub where a diverse range of physical and energetic pathways intersect. It has the capacity to influence all our functions in both body and mind. When we train our mind to stay in the present moment with positive thinking, our heart benefits both emotionally and physically. There is the old adage from the Egyptian Culture about the heart and the feather. It was believed that in order to enter the afterlife, your heart had to be light. If your heart was as light as a feather, you had passed the test of Ma'at and you entered your afterlife. However, if your heart was heavy, it was thrown to the lions, who would move in swiftly and devour it.[3] Ma'at was an Egyptian goddess that represented the Ancient Egyptian concepts of balance, order, truth and harmony, to name a few. This mythological representation illustrates that our heart is deeply affected by our thoughts and emotions, positive and negative. Negativity is the most harmful: fear, anger, grief, jealousy, worry, hatred, and self-righteousness. Whereas, positivity is the most beneficial: love, compassion, joy, and selfless action.

### Kidneys

The job of the kidneys is to remove waste and extra fluid from the blood. The kidneys take urea out of the blood and combine it with water and other substances to make urine. In Traditional Chinese Medicine, the kidneys are associated with vitality. They have been referred to as the "essence of life" because their functioning is critical to sustaining reproductive function, growth and development, and maturation.

The kidneys are also involved with the lungs in water metabolism and respiration. Psychologically, by enhancing our willpower, removing fearful thoughts, gaining more confidence, and being connected with a nourishing community, we keep kidney function happy and healthy.

### Lungs

The lungs are responsible for removing oxygen from the air we breathe and transferring it to our blood where it can be sent to our cells. The lungs also remove carbon dioxide, which we exhale. In Traditional Chinese Medicine, the lungs control breath and energy, and assist the heart with the circulation of blood. The Internal Medicine Classic states: "Energy is the commander of blood; when energy moves, blood follows." Here we see that when the lungs are not functioning optimally, the whole immune system goes out of balance—including the cellular immunity and neurohormonal immunity, which refers to both the physical and psychological components of the immune system.[4] Our lung energy declines when we experience emotions of sadness or grief. So we want to keep our lung energy uplifted to have clear thinking and creative expression.

### Liver

The liver, our "metabolic factory," is responsible for filtering, detoxifying, nourishing, replenishing, and storing blood. The liver stores large amounts of sugar in the form of glycogen, which is released into the bloodstream as glucose whenever the body requires extra infusions of metabolic energy. The liver receives all amino acids extracted from food via the small intestine, and recombines them to synthesize the various forms of protein required for growth and repair of our body tissues.

The liver also controls the peripheral nervous system, which regulates muscular activity and tension. The inability to relax is often caused by liver dysfunction or an imbalance in energy. Did you ever feel agitated to the point of heating up? That is an indication of stagnated liver energy.

Liver energy controls ligaments and tendons, which work with the muscles to regulate motor activity, and determine physical co-ordination. Liver function is reflected externally in the condition of fingernails and toenails, and by the health of eyes and vision. Blurry vision is often a result of liver malfunction rather than an eye problem. Western medicine also recognizes the symptomatic yellow eyes and skin of liver jaundice.

A healthy liver supports our optimal growth and development, balanced drive, controlled desires, ambitions, and creativity. When our liver energy is not functioning properly, we may experience intense feelings of frustration, rage, and anger. These emotions, in turn, further disrupt "liver energy" and suppress liver function in a vicious, self-destructive cycle.

Since the liver detoxifies, stores, and metabolizes what we put in our mouth, it is important to give an overview of the essential functions, because it is within our reach to work directly with this organ.

As a detoxifier, the liver processes food, herbs, drugs, toxins, and chemicals—anything that comes through our digestive system—and it can either neutralize or convert them to be excreted in a nontoxic form. For example, the liver's detoxification pathway changes a toxin, that is initially fat-soluble, to one that is water-soluble for easier excretion by the kidneys.

The liver also stores vitamins and minerals (vitamins B12, A, D, E, K; iron, zinc, manganese, copper, and molybdenum). It combines niacin and glutamic acid to make it possible for us to tolerate glucose and combines other nutrients to make antioxidants that protect our other organs.

As a metabolizer, the liver manufactures cholesterol, the basic molecule from which our adrenal hormones and our sex hormones—estrogen and testosterone—are produced. It also governs the metabolic control of carbohydrates and proteins and the regulation of the levels of glucose and amino acids in the blood.

The liver is responsible for the breakdown of sugar between meals and during times when food is not available, such as when we're asleep. It absorbs oxygen and nutrients from the blood to keep metabolic reactions working properly. Responsible for hundreds of biochemical processes, the liver is one of the most important organs in the body when it comes to health. If it functions improperly, so do we. Yet many of us abuse our liver. We overload it with fats or alcohol, bombard it with chemically processed foods, and saturate it with sugar. We also hold onto harmful patterns of thinking, such as anger and frustration, that produce excess heat in the liver.

Eating "clean" food, rich in vitamins and minerals, as well as phytochemical compounds—biologically active compounds found in plants—is the way to a healthy liver. Most importantly, having positive and loving thoughts support its function. To support healthy liver activity and to aid in its detoxification, I advise adding special nutrients to your diet, such as bioflavonoids, vitamins C, E, B1, B2, B3, and B5, and folic acid. Herbs also support liver functions, which is why the *Radiance Diet* includes bitter herbs like milk thistle, beet greens, dandelion, and ginger. Occasionally, in tandem, I will also recommend herbs that support thyroid function, since thyroid regulates our overall metabolism.

I also emphasize not to eat late at night nor graze throughout the day. The "factory" needs periodic cleaning to function optimally. Maintaining liver and biochemical balance with good food and positive thinking habits can be done every day; it should be as natural as walking.

Biochemistry, with an emphasis on physiology, was the subject of my academic career. I came to understand that irregular dietary habits of mono-dieting, binging on sugar, irregular fasting, as well as emotional swings, have a direct effect on liver health. Years later, after studying Traditional Chinese Medicine, I understand that when liver *qi* (the subtle energy) is stagnant all sorts of problems occur. In fact, one of the biggest problems that menopausal women face is stagnant liver *qi*. There are other issues, but this was my pattern. So I began to work on moving my liver *qi* using proper diet and herbs, which cooled the irritation and anger. I learned that there is a feedback loop; We get angry and heat our liver, or our liver gets stuck and we become angry. The body and mind are one, so each one influences the other. Most women have benefited when I have helped them with foods and herbs for liver support. Their energy and moods come back into balance.

I have put together a plan that focuses on the interaction of food and thought on liver function and overall digestive health. My personal plan has varied over the years due to changes that occur as I age, as well as the climates and situations that I find myself navigating. My overall plan is to eat two meals per day, with at least one of them freshly prepared with herbs and spices that support my constitution. Since I love sweets, I don't cut out desserts. Instead I allow them once or twice a week. I make sure my foods are as clean and clear of pesticides and preservatives as possible. I also include yoga postures in the morning, along with breathing and meditation.

It takes about ten days to two weeks on the *Return to Radiance* program to improve energy and strength. You may notice your eyes becoming clearer, your skin glowing, and your overall stamina increasing. I personally have found it takes about ten days for me to start seeing some benefits from a new routine. During those rare occasions when I was coming off an unbalanced diet, it would take me about two months to regain the energy and the healthy feeling that I was looking for. I know things are working in balance when I rise from my bed in the morning feeling rested and encouraged about getting started on my day. The best part is that I look forward to nourishing my body with good food, and my mind with meditation.

When we find that place of balance within our own Self, we are accessing our inner luminosity; we are returning to radiance.

———————O———————

## What Are the Foods that Give Us Energy—and Why?

We get food energy ultimately from the sun. Plants take water and carbon dioxide from the air and capture the energy from the sun, forming carbohydrates and releasing oxygen. *Carbohydrates* found in grains, fruits, vegetables, and legumes are what I call "favorable carbohydrates." (The carbohydrates found in refined sugar, cakes, pastries, and white flour products are what I call "unfavorable carbohydrates.") Carbohydrates are our quickest source of energy and assist the body in metabolizing proteins and fats. For example, fats require carbohydrates to break them down in the liver.

*Fats* are found in a number of sources; they can even be produced from eating an excess of carbohydrates. We need fat in our diet primarily for membrane function, digestion, and lubrication, but an over-abundance is unhealthy.

Foods rich in fat are milk and butter, cheese, vegetable oils, nuts, and meat. Our heart uses fatty acids as fuel, but not all fats are metabolized or "burned" so easily. They tend to clog our arteries and overload our cells, which then lose their vital energy. The best choices are to eat wild salmon, wild game, avocados, almonds, pecans, pumpkin, pine, and sunflower seeds as a source of fat. Unfortunately, the traditional American diet is made up of 30% to 40% of the "bad" fats. Why do we tend to like them so much? Perhaps we have acquired a "taste" for these substances and become habituated to think that they taste good and will satisfy our appetite. That could be why fast foods are so much in demand. Beware! Fast and synthetic foods are seriously unhealthy.

Next to water, *proteins* are the most abundant substances in our bodies. They are our major building blocks, essential for the growth and development of all body tissue. During digestion, protein is broken down into amino acids by stomach acids mixed with enzymes from the pancreas. The amino acids are then absorbed by the intestine and travel in the bloodstream to the liver. Here they are used to synthesize new body proteins to be used for the formation of hormones, enzymes (molecules necessary for many biochemical reactions), and other substances used to regulate metabolism. In times of starvation, protein stored in the body can be broken down and used for energy. When excess protein is consumed but not utilized, it is converted to fat in the liver.

The major sources of animal protein are meat, fish, poultry, eggs, and milk; plant protein sources are soy, legumes, nuts, and seeds. As with all food groups, make sure that you don't consume any of these excessively. Unlike other energy fuels, protein has no storage forms independent of function—in other words, excess protein consumed is usually stored as fat, while the surplus of the amino acids is excreted. Too much animal protein in the system puts a strain on all organs. Proteins are, in effect, a fuel of "last resort," even though they are being touted as an optimal fuel source in keto diets.

Our conventional notion of a balanced diet has changed from decade to decade as we trend from "paleo" to "keto." They seem to be promoting the best health, weight loss, longevity, and anti-aging. What was good yesterday, though, may be replaced today by a soundbite advertising the latest diet. We must keep in mind that each person has their own unique digestive ability—to absorb, utilize, and eliminate—and what works for one person, might not work for another. We do know that wild, hormone-free animal products are healthier than products from animals raised in an industrial system. Likewise, we know that fresh food is better for us than canned food. Comparative studies in the past have shown, for example, that hormone levels of insulin were different after subjects consumed a meal of fresh beans versus canned beans.

The *Radiance Diet* includes whole grains, vegetables, fruits, nuts and seeds, mineralized salt, sea vegetables, legumes, and free-range eggs, and seafood (not farm-raised with hormones). You can add some hormone-free dairy, and a little meat, but eliminate processed foods as much as possible. Keep in mind that many food production companies choose to use chemicals to keep weeds and pests from destroying their crops; they add more artificial nutrients to the earth, subsequently killing the natural biome of the soil. There are three different kinds of pesticides: herbicides, insecticides, and fungicides. All three of these pesticides are used to kill different kinds of pests found in agriculture, and even in our neighbors' gardens. These chemicals do indeed affect our food, and in many cases have injurious effects on the health of the entire planet; there is no denying this. The human body recognizes chemicals as toxic agents; the ingestion of these agents through eating and breathing causes severe stress in the system. As a result of ingesting these chemicals, the liver cannot do its work properly, which leads to increased aging and deterioration of the immune system, and causes damage to the brain and nervous system.

What about sugar? Here, moderation is essential. White sugar, the kind we should avoid the most, is devoid of the vitamins and minerals necessary for it to be properly digested. Instead, we rely on our nutrient stores to supply energy for the digestive work; as a result, our vitamin and mineral stores become depleted. Sugar in its natural state (not stripped of its minerals), is actually quite nourishing to all of our cells. The problem is that we don't have access to whole unadulterated sugar; production practices have stripped, bleached, and packaged it, making this "food" a poison to our organism. It's best to avoid white sugar, as it suppresses the immune system by causing the pancreas to secrete abnormally high quantities of insulin. This action causes the adrenal gland to become depleted. The body reacts to sugar overload the same way it reacts to stress; it creates what I call "food stress." Since processed carbohydrates like white flour, candy, pastries, and cookies are "unnatural," the body perceives them as a threat; it registers them as toxins. Eat too much sugar, and you're prone to many of the ailments associated with decreased vitality: lethargy, fatigue, candida, obesity, cardiac disease, diabetes, and many of the Western world's diet-related diseases. Complex sugars, on the other hand—those found in unadulterated sugar cane, whole grains, vegetables, and fruits—have the requisite vitamins, minerals, fiber, and water for proper digestion.

As we have just learned, when the body borrows essential vitamins and minerals to metabolize sugar, its vital reserves become depleted. This can also lead to food cravings and eating binges since the body feels the need to replenish what it has lost when digesting sugar. Excess sugar is converted into fat (*triglycerides*) by our liver, and the result for us is often depressed moods, and usually decreased vitality. I have noticed that my energy level declines within fifteen minutes of consuming a cookie. I have trained myself to remember this whenever I get the urge to eat some cookies.

———○———

Herbs are an essential supplement to your diet. More can be found on this in chapter nine and the appendices. I have recommended flower essences, as well. Flower essences are liquid formulations made by floating flowers in a bowl of water placed in the sun.[5] The idea behind these essences is that the "energy" of the flower transfers to the solution. One theory is that flowers contain a subtle, vibrational energy that resonates with human feelings and emotions. Another theory is that the essences can alter electrical impulses that affect messenger molecules in the body's psycho-neuroimmune system. I believe that there is a scientific basis for the effectiveness of flower essences, making them suitable for treating specific emotional or psychological issues, such as fear, anger, anxiety, and even low self-esteem. They can also provide soothing and nurturing support for stress and transitions in life. Each flower has its own unique properties and the mind, body and spirit are eased by their use.

Flower essences are a key part of traditional healing systems in India, Tibet, China, Japan, and Indonesia. The Vedas, among the oldest written texts, talk of treating illnesses with flowers, and the Aborigines of Australia still use fresh flowers in their hot-coal saunas, a practice some 10,000 years old. Flower essences do not have chemical constituents as measured in Western scientific standards, yet they can affect the nervous system, and thus emotions, thoughts, and feelings.

The appendices contain a list of flower essences and their specific benefits, including properties that deal with immune system disturbances. They are not a mandatory part of my program, but I encourage you to do the research on your own and try them.

We have seen that the biochemical body depends on good nutrition, and that good nutrition is most effective when combined with proper breathing and exercise. It is time now to get specific and discuss biochemistry as it pertains to disease prevention, stress reduction, mood regulation, and aging radiantly.

## THE BIOCHEMISTRY OF DISEASE PREVENTION

Everything we do directly affects our vital energy. To be healthy, all of our systems—as well as the interaction between the mind and body—must be in balance and must flow smoothly. If we lose balance for an extended period of time and the flow of our systems are interrupted, disease will be the result.

The hub of our immune system is in our gut, and it is the first line of defense against virus, bacteria, cancer cell formation, and other invaders—in a word, disease.[6] The bidirectional communication that occurs between our gut and our brain determines the health and wellbeing of our entire mind-body matrix. This communication affects the health of our lymphatic vessels and organs (thymus, spleen, tonsils, lymph nodes), white blood cells, and other specialized cells and serum factors. Since many diseases come from pathogens in our environment, the immune system's job via our gut microbiome is to protect our bodies from harmful environmental poisons and discard them.

When our immune system is compromised by poor diet, lack of exercise, fatigue, alcohol, drugs, or negative and fearful thinking, it becomes weakened; consequently, we are more vulnerable to the pathogens that create disease. How do you know if you have a healthy immune system? Ask yourself how often you catch a cold, or how often you feel run-down or tired. If your answer is "a lot," then you need to make some changes in your diet, your exercise program, your way of thinking, your way of life—or all four.

Here are the warning signs:

*Stage One:* Organ Aggravation. Here you see changes in your body: digestive disturbances, fatigue, weakness, lethargy, overly emotional responses to ordinary events. The key trademark of this stage is digestive disturbances that may include a lot of gas or bowel changes like diarrhea or lack of daily elimination.

*Stage Two:* Accumulation. At this stage, the imbalance starts to spread, and now it goes beyond the area where it first started. It may manifest in the skin at this point, or as a cold, or as swollen lymph nodes.

*Stage Three:* Infiltration. Now you start to see changes in the physiological mechanism that constitute the operations of your body. Here you will see increased blood pressure, blood sugar, and triglyceride levels.

*Stage Four:* Changes in Cellular Structure. At this stage, the process is now labeled as a disease and designated as either early-stage or later stage.

*Stage Five:* Manifest as Physical Deformity. At this stage, there is a change in the body's physical structure; the process is embedded in this structure.

**My advice:** Pay attention to symptoms outlined in Stage One; make some changes in your lifestyle that will balance your body and mind. It is easiest to heal any ailment at this stage, however, this is also the easiest stage to ignore. If you slip into Stage Two, find someone who can recognize what is taking place and can support you with holistic modalities. If you reach Stage Three before recognizing that you need to change, align yourself with several holistic-minded practitioners that will get to the issue using a multi-dimensional approach.

There are two essential steps to take when conquering the disease state:

1. Remove what is causing the issue.
2. Restore Function:
   a. Strengthen the immune system through diet, exercise, herbs, vitamins, homeopathy,[7] breathing and meditation practices.
   b. Upgrade the body's ability to remove toxins by strengthening the mechanisms of detoxification through all systems in the body, especially the liver and digestive system.
   c. Treat the disease with herbs, supplements, and other medicinal compounds that deal specifically with the disease state.

In this book, you will find the diet to help you at this critical stage of imbalance. Add the herbs and supplements specific to your needs—their traditional uses and properties are referenced in the appendices. The exercises I've included here are primarily for vitality and rejuvenation (walking, biking, swimming, and jogging are also effective). Movement and exercise support the immune system by bringing new oxygen and blood flow into the cells. Too much exercise, on the other hand, can deplete the body's nutrients, so stop just before you become tired. Finally, take time to heal and nourish yourself with meditation. Meditation improves immune function and helps to rewire your brain, leading to positive emotions.

For upgrading your immunity, cut down on cold foods, sugars, gluten (if you are subject to a reaction), harmful fats, and particularly alcohol and chemically-processed foods. Eat right, breathe in balance, and exercise with purpose; your immune system will be up-regulated, and your liver will be operating at full efficiency.

## THE BIOCHEMISTRY OF STRESS REDUCTION

Stress occurs when we are out of balance. This imbalance leads to biochemical changes within our organ systems.

When we experience stress, our bodies' reactions come from either sympathetic nervous system dominance, which produces a fight-or-flight response, or a freezing response where we become immobile. Sometimes there is a mixture of both. Ultimately, we can control these reactions, since the autonomic nervous system

(ANS) has a direct role in our response to stress. We will discuss this later.

When you digest food, when your heart beats, when your kidneys make urine, or your liver regulates metabolism, it's all controlled by the autonomic nervous system. Any disruption to the ANS system caused by stress can lead to malfunctions of your body's ordinary processes. Under stress, your body is in a constant state of imbalance, and its functions—fighting off environmental toxins or digesting and metabolizing food—can temporarily shut down.

When we undergo stress, the activated sympathetic nervous system causes the adrenal glands (located above the kidney) to secrete the stress hormones, namely, catecholamines and corticosteroids. These hormones cause the body to release its stored energy, thereby elevating fat and cholesterol levels in the blood, among other metabolites. The stress hormones break down the cells of the intestinal tract, depress the immune system by inhibiting the function of white blood cells, decrease lymphocyte production, and may cause shrinkage of the thymus gland, as well as initiating other catabolic events.[8-11]

The other component of the autonomic nervous system, the parasympathetic nervous system (PNS), works to calm the body down. To counter the fight-or-flight response, this system encourages the body to "rest and digest." Blood pressure, breathing rate and hormone flow return to normal levels as the body settles into homeostasis, or equilibrium, once more.[12]

The sympathetic and parasympathetic nervous systems work together to maintain and balance normal body function. When we are out of balance, we can experience functional loss due to the underutilization of the body's resources. Muscles begin to atrophy due to underuse. For example, the heart may become enlarged due to a lack of exercise. Illnesses associated with a nervous system imbalance may include chronic fatigue, anxiety, depression, and possibly some forms of cancer.

If you are feeling stressed, my program will provide tools to increase your resilience. (Note: there may not always be an immediate, recognizable cause; the stress may be an old habit pattern.) A proper diet creates physical and emotional changes which can then lead to biochemical balance. Examples: fruits and vegetables containing phytonutrients that balance hormone production; foods rich in calcium and magnesium like beans, nuts and all manner of greens are particularly good aids to relaxation; and seaweed nourishes the nervous, immune, and hormonal systems, and supports detoxification pathways.

Gotu kola and ginkgo stimulate the brain tissues, thereby supporting the expanding consciousness and comprehension, while simultaneously calming the mind. Herbs identified as *adaptogens*—ginseng, ashwagandha, and shatavari—are principal in helping the body deal with stress.

Exercise, including Yoga and Tai Chi Chuan, helps you to release some of the inner tension caused by stress and opens energy channels that affect both body and mind. When combined with proper breathing, exercise balances the nervous system by relieving tension. In general, exercise enhances circulation and supports the removal of harmful neurochemicals produced by the body under stress.

Breath is particularly important. Deep, diaphragmatic breathing brings the body to a state of relaxation; it will provide your cells with the extra oxygen and subtle energy needed for rebuilding.

Meditation is one of the most useful tools for changing our perceptions and moves us from a place of *reaction* to *response*. As you practice meditation, the situations that have caused tension and irritation will begin to have less impact on you. The result is a more calm and balanced way of living. You will be able to take action instead of reacting to your environment.

Stress is a relatively new phenomenon, brought on by the rhythms of a society geared toward speed, production, and success. Endocrinologist Hans Selye, who is considered one of the pioneers of stress research, first initiated the use of the term *stress* after he completed his medical training at the University of Montreal in the 1920's. By 1936, *stress* first became identified with people. Over seventy years later, our society is today faced with widespread addiction to data devices; we see how rampant this tension is in our daily lives. Stress is a result of how we view and perceive modern life; we must address it. My advice? Take time to evaluate your current lifestyle and begin to create a space where you can remain calm and healthy. The outcome will be well worth the effort.

## THE BIOCHEMISTRY OF RADIANT AGING

The body degenerates when its ability to repair itself falls behind the breakdown of its own biochemical processes. We all know young people who seem aged, and seniors who seem youthful.

Return to Radiance

Our chronology is not as important in the aging process as is having a sound mind and a healthy body.

For most people, progressive degeneration of body functions seems to be the norm with aging. The process of decline accelerates both physically and mentally if we lead a toxic lifestyle and live in a polluted environment. As we age, it seems that recovering from illness or physical injury takes longer, but why? Scientific reasoning is still out on why this happens, but several leading theories can help explain why we take longer to restore our function as we age. One of them is called the *free radical theory*. The concept speculates that either the body is generating more free radicals, or the body loses the ability to dispose of them.[13]

Free radicals are a byproduct of normal cell function. When cells create energy, they also produce unstable oxygen molecules. Free radicals are unstable oxygen molecules with unpaired electrons; their chemistry is altered when paired with other molecules. Generated during the metabolic process, they can attack membranes, the enzyme systems, and even your DNA. Free radicals can also develop in the body from exposure to toxic chemicals in the air, food, or water; radiation from X-rays and sunlight; cured meats, alcohol, herbicides, drugs, nicotine, or stress. As soon as they are produced, free radicals are highly toxic and sequestered by antioxidants. Overproduction of free radicals results in a cascade effect, and more are formed. Our system eliminates most, but not all.

An antioxidant is defined as any substance that delays or inhibits oxidative damage to the tissues. They exist as part of the liver's detoxification system. Antioxidants, like coenzyme Q10 and melatonin, are also manufactured by the body and serve as natural antioxidants. Our antioxidant defense system needs vitamins and minerals that come from the food we eat, particularly selenium, copper, zinc, vitamin E, and vitamin C. Oxidation is a process that occurs when something rusts. We need to create a health program that will 'prevent rust' by including an array of antioxidants as well as clean lifestyle habits that will not harm our body. There is some evidence that suggests we can only get the full antioxidant benefits from eating plants and other foods. Supplements appear to be less effective. No matter how far along you are in the aging process, start now. Remember, you have the precious amalgam within your own biochemistry that will rejuvenate you, so use it!

Keep these tips in mind:

- Overnight fasting enhances the brain and the immune system by facilitating cell renewal and enhanced capacity for your body to fight off foreign invaders. Don't eat after 7 p.m.
- Eat less, live longer. By decreasing your caloric intake, you will not only lengthen your lifespan, but you will have a healthier brain and mind.
- Organically-grown raw fruit and vegetable juices are the best source of organic vitamins and minerals.
- Include good fats in your diet. Polyunsaturated fats and trans-fats produce toxins that affect your brain and nervous system and create free radicals. When you do eat fat, choose cold-pressed, unrefined oils like olive, coconut, peanut, sunflower or sesame; included in this list is ghee.

- Avoid processed foods as well as other foods that have chemicals in them—sweeteners, artificial coloring, natural flavorings, etc. Our environment is toxic enough as it is, why add to the burden placed on your liver?

- Include organic or pesticide-free raw fruits and vegetables in your diet. They contain the best source of organic substances that repair and nourish cells.

- Include fiber by eating whole unadulterated grains and legumes (organic and non GMO as much as possible). They keep the bowels clean and act like a broom to sweep out toxic substances.

- Add carotenoids to the vitamins mentioned above, particularly beta-carotene. Carotenoids are found in green leafy vegetables, carrots and sweet potatoes.

- Flavonoids, found in fruits and vegetables, neutralize free radicals and potentiate vitamin C.

- Resveratrol found in red wine and Japanese knotweed has been shown to slow the aging process.

- Avoid snacking. Give your digestive system a rest between meals. Snacking increases aging by keeping the digestive engines running all day long.

- Get up and go with exercise. Movement allows energy to circulate and not stagnate. The old bromide "use it or lose it" is true for all parts of your body, particularly your brain.

- Meditate as nature intended. "Seal the senses and focus the mind" is the prescription for a vital brain and a radiant life.

# THE BIOCHEMISTRY OF BETTER MOODS

A look at how our biochemical networks communicate is necessary if we are going to understand the reasons why we may be happy, sad, nervous, anxious or experience any emotion. The chemistry of the brain has continued to intrigue me because I have always been interested in improving my ability to focus and remain calm.

As human beings, we are privileged to have the largest cerebral cortex of all mammals, relative to the size of our brain. Some whales have larger brains than we do; however, ours are more complex and have a more convoluted neocortex. Our neocortex, capable of complex processes, requires masterful communication networks. Our ability to connect to our environment via our sensory and synaptic brain channels allows us to process information, feelings, solve problems, and move with intention. It allows us to make decisions (sometimes easier said than done), store memories (the good with the bad), learn something new, and do all of the things that make us human. Our brains are the coordinators of information, from all of our five senses to the mind itself.

Humans have the ability of self-awareness, something which is absent in animals. Our brains' capability to send messages in the neuronal forest, with speeds of up to 120 miles per hour on the synapses, is quite intriguing. So, if you are not fired up, neurologically speaking, you might not feel at your best. The human mind suffers from distraction, disturbance, and fatigue daily; these tendencies can decrease our capacity to be radiant. I often recommend that my students "use their body as feedback" to become aware of the integration of body and mind. Your body responds to all of your feelings and thoughts and houses your emotions. Any tightness or pain you are physically experiencing can be used as a signal to detect the location of your energy blockages. When used in combination with attention to your thoughts and emotions, you will receive significant feedback to gain focus and stability in your life. Over time, you can even change how your mind sends messages to the rest of your body. For example, when you experience physical or mental discomfort, don't ignore or suppress it; instead, find its source. One of the most profound "ah-ha" moments came to a client of mine who suffered from fatigue and a lack of focus.

"Elizabeth" complained that she would be drowsy and drift off during the day because she was so tired.

"Are you aware of when you begin to feel this?" I asked her.

"I find myself somewhat depressed at the start of the day, and then as the day carries on, I get drowsy," she answered.

"Do you have any idea why you might feel depressed? Are you eating any foods that cause you to feel sleepy?" I continued.

"I am not sure, but probably?" She hesitated.

"Are you taking any time to rest and digest the experiences of your day when you get home?"

"Are you kidding?" she laughed. " I already have to deal with my husband, the kids, the dog, and everything else; that will just create more of a stress on me."

"Elizabeth, I think if you want to resolve this issue, we need to get to the root of it so that we can begin to restore your energy."

"Well, I have gotten this far, why not give it a try," she said.

We set a schedule for her to work with some suggested changes, then chose a time to meet and re-evaluate her progress.

I recommended that Elizabeth pay close attention to what she ate daily for lunch, and to take a walk after eating, say for about fifteen minutes. Also, I gave her a relaxation practice and advised her to pay attention to when she found herself beginning to drift off and wanting to sleep. These exercises, integrated with an assigned diaphragmatic breathing practice, became her foundation stones. Over time, by combining physical practices with assessing her thoughts at the time of drowsiness, Elizabeth understood what was causing her melancholy, tiredness, and drowsiness.

———○———

Our neurotransmitters—the chemical messengers that serve to transfer information in our brain's networks—do indeed affect how we feel and how we think. Anyone suffering from deficient serotonin, dopamine, or GABA can attest to this.

How we feel and think affects our neurotransmitters, creating physical changes in our brain. Our neurotransmitter balance or imbalance reflects how emotionally and mentally resilient and stable we are, and ultimately how well we can remain calm and focused. These chemical messengers also regulate the brain's ability to grow new cells—neurogenesis—which affects how we process information. A little background information in neuroscience will help us get started on the journey to bring our brain to its greatest vitality.

Neurotransmitters need to be synthesized by our bodies. So how do these neurotransmitters work and have potential to affect our mood? A brief overview of how communication takes place, may be in order, to see where problems can occur. Your brain is essentially like a series of electrical connections. Neurons are the wires that carry the signal in a specific pattern to different parts of the brain. They connect to other neurons through terminals known as *synapses*. It is at these synapses that the main signal of the neuron, the "electrical charge," is transmitted by release of neurotransmitters from one neuron into the synapse. These neurotransmitters include serotonin, dopamine, GABA, glutamate and norepinephrine, and others that are not included in this discussion. These molecules are dumped into the synapse where they bind (like a key going into a lock) to a receptor on a second neuron. This "binding" causes the signal to be transmitted from neuron A to neuron B. Any deficiency in these neurotransmitters hampers the brain's function and ability to send messages. The synthesis of some of these neurotransmitters requires dietary amino acids as well as micronutrients that support their transformation. Therefore, ingesting a diet with sufficient amino acids, as well as vitamins and minerals, becomes important for maintaining neurological function.

There are many substances, over fifty, that can be classified as neurotransmitters. For the purpose of this section, I will focus on three classical ones that we find in the field of neuropsychiatry. We can see that to create focus and the ability to stay sharp, it requires us to have a balanced amount of norepinephrine and dopamine. To uplift our mood and change our pain perception requires serotonin. To foster calmness and tranquility requires GABA—gamma aminobutyric acid.

## *Dopamine*

Dopamine, an excitatory neurotransmitter, plays a key role in the brain's ability to experience joy, happiness, and maintain focus and concentration. Its networks are extensive, reaching three main areas of the brain. First, there is the frontal cortex, which is the area of the brain responsible for cognitive function, focus, and working memory. Second, is the limbic system in the brain where emotions are processed. And third, is the striatum, the area that assists us in voluntary movement. Dopamine is also implicated in our reward systems. Many of us have experienced the effects of caffeine on our brain, for example. Being awake and alert—the rewards—cause us to crave more.

## *Serotonin*

This neurotransmitter is a calming one. It is a well-known neurotransmitter because it is believed to be important in feeling happy, content, and relaxed. Low serotonin levels are associated with depression. While the dopamine system is stimulating, serotonin has an opposite effect, especially on appetite—a Yin Yang dichotomy.

What fascinates me is that 90% of serotonin is not made in the brain, but is made in the enterochromaffin cells in the gut. Here it is responsible for our intestinal health, regulation of vascular functions, and intestinal movement. The remainder of serotonin is synthesized in the brain by the serotonergic neurons. Nicholas Giarmin, a professor of pharmacology, and Daniel Freedman, a professor of psychiatry at Yale University School of Medicine, both confirmed that the human brain manufactures serotonin at various sites within the brain. They found that the Pineal Gland contains 3140 ng (nanograms) of serotonin per gram of tissue, unmistakably the richest site of serotonin in the brain! This discovery implies the Pineal Gland is an important site of serotonergic activity.[14]

We can assume this is the reason Yoga Science places emphasis on focusing our attention at the Ājñā Chakra—the home of the pineal gland. With specific breathing and meditation practices, we gain access to this area and work with our ability to focus. In other words, we move inward, by-passing our sensory stimulation.

We now know that the serotonin system plays an important role in our ability to modulate and cope with stress, as well as temper our emotional behavior. Some speculate that any impairment in the system, due to genetic predisposition, for example, can result in less resilience both physically and mentally in stressful situations. We know that when a person is under stress, the hormones released into the nervous system impede the proper functioning of the brain pathways.

### GABA and Glutamate

GABA (gamma amino butyric acid) is associated with anxiety reduction, and allows "stimulating" signals to be turned off. It is responsible for our sense of tranquility. GABA is extremely important because it serves to inhibit or turn off rapid signals that occur in nerve transmission. It is also referred to as an *inhibitory chemical* or a key to anxiety reduction. Glutamate, the companion to GABA, is an excitatory neurotransmitter that stimulates us. When glutamate is converted into GABA, it behaves much like a yin/yang relationship. Thus our perception (the ability to organize and interpret sensory information) is influenced by the balance between GABA and glutamate.[15]

What happens in the brain when we are calm and tranquil? The effect of sitting quietly and relaxing are profound. The deep state of rest changes the neurochemical transmission in our brain. Each of these naturally-occurring brain chemicals has been linked to different aspects of how we feel. I would also like to mention that when we meditate, all of these neurochemicals come into play, but there are two specific ones worth noting. The first, oxytocin, is a pleasure hormone that reduces tension and anxiety. It is the hormone responsible for bonding between a mother and child. Interestingly, C. Sue Carter's research with bluebirds and with prairie voles revealed oxytocin is also linked with monogamy.[16]

The second set of neurochemicals, endorphins, are the chemicals that create the exhilarating feeling commonly referred to as "the runner's high." They are responsible for feeling vital and happy.

Positive emotions and thoughts elicit a different group of chemicals than when we are negative. An angry and agitated state causes stress; stress creates inflammation, both emotionally and physically. As a result, when we feel this type of stress over a long duration it results in visible brain tissue shrinkage. Evidently, negative emotions create a "hurt" or "ill" response in the brain, similar to sitting in the sun too long and becoming sunburned.

You can observe how your brain sends molecular messages to your body based on your perceptions, thoughts, and feelings, exactly matching the emotion with the proper chemical response.

For example, when you feel anxious, your immune system down-regulates and eventually weakens, because the stress response initially prepares your body for the fight or flight. Over long periods, however, the chemicals released have adverse reactions to the healthy cells. When you are happy, though, you send a different set of immune-communicating molecules coursing through your bloodstream. The message is clear: be positive and productive in your thinking so you can nourish your radiant mind.

———————O———————

Hormones are chemical messengers that affect all of our cells. You can see how vital hormones are when you experience changes—e.g., low thyroid function, loss of estrogen, high testosterone. In the next chapter, you'll learn how hormones work and why the *Return to Radiance* program will keep them balanced.

CHAPTER 4

————————○————————

# Hormones: Our Metabolic Messengers

*When you shift your perspective to see the signs of balance and*
*imbalance through the lenses of wisdom and compassion, you will*
*have begun to listen to the teacher within—your inner guide.*

Hormones are chemicals that stimulate cells or tissues into action. Hormones travel through the blood and throughout your body; therefore, they have an effect on many organs at the same time.

Hormones are one of the most important energy-support systems that we have. Everything in the body functions or malfunctions based on our hormone production, secretion, and circulation. Some of the best ways I know to keep hormones flowing freely are following a good diet, sequenced movement, and meditation practice. Ultimately, the mind has more effect on hormonal flow; it is far better to be stress-free and instead cultivate positive thoughts and relationships.

---○---

In my own life, there was a time when I had ended a relationship, began a new job and moved to a new "uninviting" city. I became unknowingly stressed. I say unknowingly because I knew there was stress, yet I did not understand the degree of stress I was going through. Usually when under stress I don't notice its harmful effect, this time was different. This "stress" became known to me one day as I tried to remember a telephone number. I was in an unfamiliar small town and had to make calls to set up my new life. I could not recall the number I needed. Coincidentally, I was also working as a medical liaison in psychiatry and knew that one of side effects of stress is that the brain's hippocampus can shrink. The hippocampus is thought to be vital in learning and memory. I recognized that my memory issue was a result of the stress that I was experiencing. Shortly after this episode, my body began to show signs of decline, and my mood became depressed. I had not been attentive to my diet and was eating out often. I was struggling to keep up with the overwhelming demands of a new town and a new job in a corporate environment which was lacking in compassion. I was very unhappy with the place I had landed, both physically and mentally.

My former life was gone, this new one was vastly different, and I had to change everything in my life to accommodate my new reality. So, I stepped back and took a look at the situation. After contemplating, I realized I could not let this new situation deplete me. At that moment, I decided to take a different approach. Why not take the entire experience and flip it around to see the positive training it could provide for me? I maintained classes in Tai Chi and my practices in meditation, even though a colleague suggested that taking medication would be a better solution. I knew enough from my training that diet and meditation would help me get through this challenging time.

I don't want to claim that good habits alone will regulate mood and hormones, however they are an important part of optimal wellness. Eating foods that produce clarity and calmness in our mind and body is essential, as well as utilizing practices that include breath awareness and meditation. Over time incorporating these practices into your lifestyle will build vitality and a feeling of contentment.

―――――○―――――

We have a group of organs and glands that make up the endocrine system; it consists of eight major glands that secrete hormones into the blood. These hormones, in turn, travel to different tissues and regulate various bodily functions, such as metabolism, growth, and sexual function. In essence, these chemical messengers tell the body how to behave. Many scientists believe hormones are the most important chemicals in the body. Without them, we literally could not function.

The word *hormone* comes from the Greek word *horman,* meaning "to urge on." In a sense, that's what hormones do: they urge on the nervous system, immune system, and reproductive system, among others, so that they perform in a healthy and appropriate way. The endocrine glands and organs send messages to the brain, which in turn "signal" the hormones to enter the bloodstream. Hormones are the master regulators. Depending on which particular body function they are intended to affect, they will "stop off" at their designated cells. This could be likened to a highly sophisticated Federal Express System, delivering the correct hormone to the correct location.

While men maintain a high degree of hormonal consistency throughout their lives, women's hormonal levels go through these two phases each month:

1) hormones from the pituitary gland stimulate the follicles in the ovaries to grow in size and number and excrete estrogen in the simulated follicles; this gives rise to an ovum.

2) the ovum is released into the fallopian tube and, if no fertilization takes place, menstruation occurs.

Far greater hormonal changes occur during menopause. Interestingly, this seems to be more of a problem among women from the West rather than from other cultures. As Americans, we seem to look upon menopause as something to be dreaded—the "change of life" that brings us closer to death, a change that can take anywhere from one to ten years. In the Black Hills, however, Native Americans have a ritual to celebrate the change for three days and three nights! My friend, Ike Sayther West, shared with me that Native American women go to sacred caves in the Hills where they use nature's remedies—crystals, mosses, and herbs—to support the process. For these women, menopause is a celebrated ceremony honoring the transition from one phase of their life to another. By living a lifestyle honoring the body, mind, and heart, their practices allow these women's bodies a smoother transition.

Ike married into the Eagle Clan; they are well respected for what they know about healing. The eagle itself symbolizes balance; if an eagle loses a feather from one wing, it will lose a feather from the other.

"In your society you think of healing in terms of taking something out," Ike told me. "Removing something from the body, a germ or a cancer. To the Native Americans, this is very imbalanced. If you take something out, you must put something back. If you have an endocrine imbalance, maybe from ovarian insufficiency, a grandmother would ask: 'What have you given away? Your femininity? Your femaleness?' If the woman gets her femaleness back, there is no void to fill with disease."

Part of the aim of *Return to Radiance* is to "put something back" to restore the femininity, vitality, and radiance which has been lost through imbalance in our lives. If we give away our true essence by identifying with outer happenings, we lose our greatest asset, the Self.

————O————

Anything that causes an imbalance in either the total amount or the ratio of the secreted hormones can cause a wide range of health problems. For women, the most common problems are estrogen and progesterone imbalances and thyroid dysfunction. Even when we are going through menopause—which causes extreme fluctuations in hormones—we can find balance if we choose the right diet for both the body and mind.

Hormonal imbalances can result in digestive disturbances, mood fluctuations, fatigue, heart disease, thyroid issues and other irregularities. In general, most hormonal problems are a result of environmental toxins found in our water, air, food, and negative thinking patterns. Modern medicine makes it possible for us to alter our hormonal levels artificially through the use of manufactured hormones. In some cases, hormonal therapy may be needed if a particular gland's hormone secretions are too much, too little, or none at all. An example of this is using thyroid hormone when the thyroid levels are too low or non-existent; we need adequate levels of thyroid hormones to regulate our metabolism.

It is my view that in the past, hormonal therapy was used too often during the transitions associated with menopause. It appears the practice has lessened since medical science has shown it to be correlated with several cancers. It would be better to start with a focus on diet, proper movement, and meditation. I've seen women with many symptoms of hormonal imbalance recover by addressing the digestive function through diet alone.

—————O—————

Since this book is about radiance—the inner luminosity which occurs when we are energetic and vital—any in-depth discussion of the endocrine system is beyond this text's scope. However some of the endocrine glands that directly (or even indirectly) affect our hormonal health should at least be mentioned:

1. The *pituitary gland* controls the function of most other endocrine glands; it is sometimes referred to as "the master gland." In turn, the pituitary is controlled in large part by the hypothalamus, a region of the brain that lies just above the pituitary. Hormones from the *pituitary gland*

influence—among other things—the rate of growth, rate of metabolism, ovulation, and lactation. Deficiency in the pituitary can cause underdeveloped sexual organs, or early menopause in women, and often a drop in the level of sexual desire. The pituitary secretes a hormone called ACTH (adrenocorticotropic hormone), which plays a part in the adrenals' production of androgen, a hormone some consider to be more important to our vitality than estrogen. Here is a list of hormones associated with the pituitary gland:

**Pituitary hormones include:**

- Adrenocorticotropic Hormone (ACTH): Controls your *adrenal gland* hormones, which affect heart rate, blood pressure, and the balance of salt and water in your body
- Growth hormone (GH): Controls the speed and size at which your body grows
- Thyroid-stimulating hormone (TSH): Controls your *thyroid gland* hormones, which control how fast your body's chemical functions work
- LH and FSH: Control your sex hormones testosterone and estrogen, which affect fertility
- Prolactin: Controls the production of breast milk

2. The last endocrine gland to be discovered was the *pineal gland,* located deep in the center of the brain. Hormones from the pineal gland influence moods, sleep/wake cycles, and appetite. Melatonin, a hormone produced by

the pineal gland, is known to be particularly helpful in maintaining circadian rhythm as well as regulating our reproductive hormones. As we age, our bodies make less melatonin; its production is particularly impaired in those with Alzheimer's and other dementias.[1] No human clinical research has been done to show the direct benefits of melatonin for dementia prevention, though several trials have examined its short-term effects on cognitive function. While melatonin is not a sex hormone, per se, it does strongly contribute to maintaining our sexual functions well into our later years.

3. Hormones from the *thyroid gland* influence virtually all of our body's systems, which is why people with an underactive thyroid are often fatigued, depressed, and lacking vitality. The thyroid gland secretes thyroid hormones; T4 (*thyroxine*) is biochemically converted to T3 (*triiodothyronine*). T3 controls the speed at which the body's chemical functions happen; in other words, it controls our metabolic rate. T3 stimulates almost every tissue in the body to produce proteins and, as a result, increases the amount of oxygen our cells use.

4. Hormones of the *adrenal glands,* as mentioned before, synthesize other hormones, including our sex hormones. If our sex hormones are functioning well, they act as a buffer against stress. Perhaps the two most important hormones secreted by the adrenals are *cortisol* and *DHEA.* Cortisol is activated in response to stress, anxiety, and hypoglycemia; *DHEA* (*dehydroepiandrosterone*), an androgen, is the

precursor of our sex hormones estrogen and testosterone. High levels of DHEA are found in vibrant young people; however, the levels are not as high in those who smoke and are stressed. Currently, many in our world are experiencing the increased stress created by excessive use of social media. Under stress, our bodies don't manufacture as much DHEA; instead, they concentrate on producing what is often an excess amount of cortisol. As we age, we're told the level of DHEA decreases in our body—as is evidenced by the current societal propensity toward consumption of DHEA tablets. I believe that if we keep stress low through diet, exercise, and meditation, we'll reduce the strain on the adrenals. If we can do this, we leave the adrenal glands free to manufacture their own DHEA, thereby giving us little to no need for supplements. Since I wrote my first book, *Sexual Radiance,* new research has shown that DHEA can have positive effects on the vaginal tissue.[2] I have had several clients who deal with vaginal dryness and atrophy look to DHEA vaginal suppositories to keep their tissues vital.

5.  Hormones secreted from the *pancreas* regulate our blood-sugar concentrations. The pancreas secretes the hormones insulin and glucagon into the bloodstream. The latter is utilized when we need glucose taken out of storage, such as in between meals, and insulin is accessed after we eat and need to store glucose in our cells as glycogen. Both hormones help to regulate our energetic ups and downs during the day. When they're not regulated (when we binge

out on pastries, for example), we have a surge in insulin and drop in glucagon—with a corresponding drop in our energy that results in fatigue.

6. Hormones from the *ovaries*—estrogen and progesterone—regulate our sexual and reproductive functioning, as well as our brain and nervous system. As menopause arrives, production of estrogen and progesterone, as well as other hormones, decrease, but the female body has the capacity to make adjustments for hormonal balance throughout its lifetime. It is important to note that other body sites manufacture estrogen and progesterone, primarily the adrenal glands, digestive organs, kidneys, and liver. This is why the *Radiance Diet* is concerned with looking at the entire body. Every part of us is connected and must be in balance. We can build resilience and balance our hormones through diet, exercise, and meditation. If we pay attention to the patterns of imbalance—e.g., emotional swings—that are the result of core hormonal imbalances, we can adjust our daily routine to support our constitution. We can thus strengthen our ability to glide through the in-and-out states of balance, thereby creating resilience of the physical and subtle body.

When we move from a state of balance to imbalance, our digestive system is the first to signal us. Supporting our digestive fire strengthens the communication between the body and mind through the gut-brain network called the *enteric nervous system.* To begin strengthening the hormonal body, we must begin by working with our diet to support a strong and resilient digestive system.[3, 4]

# FOODS, PLANTS AND HORMONES

All plants contain chemicals—collectively referred to as phyto-nutrients ("Phyto" means plant), and have an impact on our hormones.[5] These chemicals are manufactured by plants throughout their lifespan, but especially during the early stages of growth. Each plant category—for example, *Brassica oleracea*, which includes broccoli, cabbage, and cauliflower—has particular chemicals that specifically affect our systems in different ways. Certain phytonutrients work as hormonal balancers. This is why we need to have a varied diet. Let's see how all foods work on hormonal function:

- Simple sugars: stress immune function and deplete our adrenal hormones
- Seafoods: contain essential minerals and have essential fatty acids that support metabolic function
- Legumes: are sources of estrogen-like compounds
- Fruits: contain bioflavonoids—plant derived compounds—which regulate hormone production
- Vegetables: contain compounds that aid in hormone production
- Sea Vegetables: are richest source of minerals especially for our thyroid function
- Grains: regulate our blood-sugar levels, which help regulate appetite

- Essential Fatty Acids: support hormone production, thyroid and adrenal activity, formation of healthy cellular membranes, and brain health

You can see that whole grains, legumes, fruits, and vegetables help to build a foundation of health and vitality, while promoting rich sources of nutrients for hormone production.

Hormones are the messengers communicating between the mind and body. When we slow down enough to become aware of their messages, we can become deeply attuned to what we specifically need. What we need is often more simple than we think. We can adopt lifestyle habits for our minds and bodies—and the hormones that govern them—to keep us in balance. When dealing with significant imbalance, it is wise to seek the guidance of a practitioner or doctor to support your healing journey; we often are unable to see ourselves objectively. When you shift your perspective to see the signs of balance and imbalance through the lenses of wisdom and compassion, you will have begun to listen to the teacher within—your inner guide.

————O————

Remember the autonomic nervous system (ANS) with its sympathetic and parasympathetic branches? Each branch stimulates the organs, and when you breathe and exercise, hormones are released from those organs helping the body functions continue to operate in a healthy way.

In the *Return to Radiance* program, we use breath awareness and exercise as a means for taking conscious control over our autonomic nervous system. Through the regulation of our breathing and the amount and type of exercise we engage in, we can bring our body and mind into total balance. Certain endocrine glands have a rich supply of neurons from both branches of the ANS; activity from these neurons controls hormonal secretion. For example, epinephrine and norepinephrine are released by the adrenal glands during stress; insulin and glucagon are manufactured by the pancreas, and so on. When we regulate our breathing patterns and exercise, we can change many of the physiological happenings in our body as well as releasing unwanted thought-patterns.

When we are stressed or scared, our breathing patterns change and our adrenal glands start producing adrenaline. While this is the correct response in a life or death situation, it is not something you want to want to occur on a regular basis.

Diaphragmatic breathing, on the other hand, is a powerful propellant for blood circulation, boosting the flow of hormones, sending them coursing through the system without causing extra work for the heart. Diaphragmatic breathing also massages our internal organs—including all of the female reproductive organs— which increases the flow of energy to the entire endocrine system. This practiced way of breathing serves to balance the mind, creating the opportunity for calmness and tranquility.

So far, I've talked mainly about chemistry and biology. However, this is only one aspect of vitality—there is also the spiritual aspect. The teachings of vital energy and radiance were first introduced by adepts in Yoga Science and Taoism in the East, and there is great wisdom to be learned from them. Even if we have no desire to embrace an entire philosophy, we can still glean skillful living practices; we can experience improvement in our lives, and receive the luminous vital energy we seek. These adepts have shared practices that have endured for thousands of years and are written in the ancient scriptures. Here in *Return to Radiance,* I will be providing knowledge and practices received from my educational training and personal experience.

PART I I

# Decoding Lessons
# from the East

Return to Radiance

# CHAPTER 5

———————○———————

# Energy Pathways

*If we look at our energy channel as a river system with
an origin, pathway, and outlet, we come to understand
and know that our body and mind operate with
the same principles found in nature.*

It has been said that we are breathing, feeling, and thinking beings. All of these functions require that we have energy. According to Yoga Science and Traditional Chinese Medicine (TCM), everything that we see on the physical level is always connected to a subtle "invisible" flow of energy. These subtle energy centers and systems within ourselves govern our physical, emotional, mental, and spiritual health and well-being. They are the foundation for energy and vitality.

The subtle energy pathways are known as the *meridians* in Chinese Medicine and *nadis* in Ayurvedic Medicine. These pathways were discovered through spiritual practices of pranayama and meditation by those ancient practitioners who were "seers" of these subtle energy channels. By allowing themselves to become deeply immersed in another state of consciousness, ancient masters could literally "see" inside the body. Due to their heightened sensitivities, these healing masters could open a deeper part of themselves to see this parallel world of the invisible. Their observations have helped us understand the interconnectiveness of this subtle energy network to the vitality in our healing force.

————O————

There are two basic principles of the universe: energy and consciousness. In Yoga Science these are called *prana shakti* and *chitta shakti*. They are the opposite poles of the same principle. Therefore, any changes in our energy can evoke changes in our consciousness, and any changes in our consciousness can evoke changes in our energy.[1] I have heard it said that we can expand our consciousness by liberating or freeing our energy. This is the principle of Yoga Science, specifically Tantra, and the basis of our study of Radiance, the luminous vital energy that dwells within us.[2]

When we work with the energy of our own mind and body through diet, movement, breath, and meditation practices, we become aware of subtle energy that flows through our body's electrical circuitry. When we collect, contain, and concentrate our energies, we are able to expand and circulate it through different energy channels in our body.

Over time, our awareness expands and we gain access to the potential which lies dormant within our own being. To reach a place of vitality where illness is destroyed and health reestablished, we must collect, contain, and focus the energy with the help of the mind. This is how we "Return to Radiance."

———○———

If we look at our energy channel as a river system with an origin, pathway, and outlet, we come to understand and know that our body and mind operate with the same principles found in nature. When we are aware of how our energy flows and where it begins and ends, we can gain access to what drives our own healing force. We will discover what nourishes us and helps us transform ourselves into luminous vital beings. When the energy flow is either impeded or exceeded, in other words, imbalanced, we experience anxiety or depression, irritability, and possible disease states. We find ourselves with a "whole body" problem.

According to the science of Ayurveda, there is an energy channel that carries the mind, called mano vaha srotas—*pathway of the mind*. It is said to be rooted in our brain, heart, and chakras. Dr. Vasant Lad, an esteemed Ayurvedic doctor, states that our mind originates in these three centers.[3] This energy channel, or pathway, is referred to as a kosha in the Yoga Tradition's text, Taittiriya Upanishad, and is said to encompass the whole person. There are five koshas, which are sheaths or layers, starting from the most subtle body layer to the gross or physical body layer. The opening of these pathways can be found in the synapses of the brain, marma points (similar to acupuncture points), and our sensory organs. We can use these openings as gateways to manipulate even the subtlest of energy, which explains why acupuncture or marma therapy works to heal our organism. With this knowledge and understanding, we can develop practices to unblock, activate, and ultimately heal ourselves.[4]

Let's take a look at the energy maps in our body.

————◯————

Our body, mind, and spirit work synergistically as an intelligent energy system that maintains its inner harmony freely and easily when it is aligned with the infinite wisdom of the universe. Each one of us possesses an intelligent energy system, a microcosm of universal intelligence, innately attuned and designed to move in sync with its vibration. You know you are in sync with the body's wisdom when your being "radiates" the essence of vitality and joy.

Joy is the emotion that is the source of radiance; vitality is its expression. The body cannot conceptualize stress, yet when we create disharmony through our thoughts, actions, poor diet, lack of movement, or misaligned relationships, the body's ability to function at optimum efficiency is compromised. When you pay attention to the subtle messages of your body and recognize what is needed, vitality improves, and joy awakens in your heart. It is necessary to have the knowledge of the inner dimensions of the body to collect, concentrate, and circulate the flow of our vital energy. Therefore, we need to review several concepts.

————◯————

According to Yoga Science, a human being is made of five sheaths, or layers of energy. As introduced above, these are called *koshas.* In many yoga texts, you'll find the five sheaths grouped into three bodies: 1) the *physical body* and *vital force*—the "gross body;" 2) the *mental body, intellect,* and *ego*—the "subtle body;" and 3) the *soul* and *spirit*—the "causal body." The koshas are recognized in many different spiritual traditions; each vibrant kosha is an experience of a different dimension in our life.

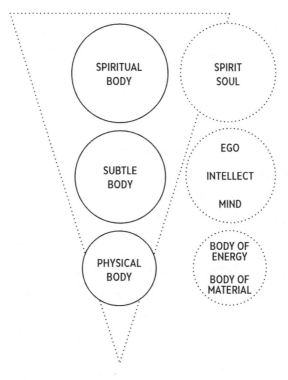

5.1 ILLUSTRATION - THE KOSHAS

If we are to be truly radiant, we need to be aware of all our bodies, as well as how to keep them cleansed, nourished, and rejuvenated. Remember, these energy layers range from the material to the subtle; I will briefly talk about each one.

## THE BODY—PHYSICAL AND VITAL FORCE

The first layer (annamaya kosha) is one you are familiar with, your physical body and energy field. This outermost layer of your physical body consists of cells, tissues, organs, bones, and muscles, as well as energy that governs your biological processes—breathing, digestion, and blood circulation.

The annamaya kosha requires food, water, and air to function, live and thrive. It is also dependent on an energetic force called *chi* in Chinese medicine, *qi* in Japanese, and *prana* in Yoga Science. The ancient Egyptians called it the *ka*. Acupuncture, marma therapy and homeopathy are healing practices based on this energy field. They don't directly work with your physical body; they affect the vital force that activates and sustains it.[5]

Although the physical body appears to be solid matter, physicists have said that it is composed of vibrating energy and subtle information that is systematically organized. When your physical body ceases to function at the time of death, your heart and lungs stop working, and your cells begin to disintegrate. The pranic energy field also begins to disintegrate since the breath carries this life force, yet it takes longer than the physical body. While this concept is not widely understood in Western Culture, due to its strong identification with the material body, there was a time when physicians were aware of this vital force.[6] It was before the birth of the relationship between pharmaceuticals and the economy; a doctor's mode of treatment when treating disease states was shifted to focus on individual symptoms rather than looking at the whole body energy system. This transition to Allopathic medicine led to the loss of knowledge and understanding of traditional healing systems. The allopathic model is now beginning to integrate some of the ancient healing modalities that can take root, and uplift our current medical system.

Without prana, or vital energy, you cannot live. When prana is moving freely, you feel awake, alive, vital, and creative. Gratefully, the ancient masters have passed down practices for cleansing, nourishing, and rejuvenating this field of energy.

The exercises in this program, including diaphragmatic breathing and alternate nostril breathing, are specifically designed to enhance optimal functioning of the pranic or vital energy field. Note: while prana is also present in food, it is the breath that is the greatest carrier.

Other forms supporting this field of matter and energy (referred to as the pranamaya kosha) include being in nature where there is clean water, fresh air, and sunlight; these are essential for maintaining the health of the vital force. Ancient medical systems recognize the sun is a source of vital energy (prana) that can be absorbed by our bodies. Plants are fed by the sun, so fresh whole foods are a major source of prana. This is why diet and nutrition are essential to reclaiming radiance.

## THE SUBTLE BODY—MIND, EGO AND INTELLECT

The next kosha, and a more subtle layer of being, is our field of thought (manomaya kosha)—the mind, ego, and intellect. This is also the level of the conscious mind—our emotions, feelings, and desires. In other words, this kosha is our day-to-day aware-ness that processes information through the utilization of our five senses. This layer serves as a bridge between the outer world and the inner world; it takes the experiences and sensations of the outside world and brings them into the intuitive fields of energy. The manomaya kosha also conveys information bidirectionally to the causal (spiritual) body, and from the causal body back to the physical body. It acts as a messenger.[7] We know by this that the mind and body are inseparable; what goes on in the mind has an impact on the body, and vice versa.

The mind is the finest instrument that you have and has broad capabilities; thoughts are its ultimate manifestation. It is, for this reason, important to train the mind because of the integral rela-tionship it has with our body and spirit. While processing input from our five senses, the untrained mind responds reflexively causing a reactive temperament, rather than a responsive one. Many people and most animals routinely operate at this level. Your mind is in constant, rapid motion unless you train it to be still, which is accomplished through the practice of meditation.

So far I have been speaking about the thoughts and ego of our lower mind, but there is a more subtle function of mind that is often translated as "intellect." The real meaning, though, is broader and encompasses all the functions of the higher mind, including intuition that leads to wisdom. The impulses emanating from the manomaya kosha are impulses of higher intelligence and vibrate with our physical layer—this creates our body's reality.

Access to this function of higher mind is what distinguishes human beings from animals. Creativity and clarity come intuitively without effort. Human beings have the privilege of directing their lives without natural instincts dominating their thinking. At this level we respond, not react. As I have mentioned, humans have the ability to see their actions and thinking patterns through a process of *self-reflection*. Animal anatomy and physiology does not support this function. The best way we can attain access to this process is through meditation and mantra. As your meditation practice deepens, the veil that covers your mind soon dissolves and you become more insightful. Self-reflection brings more clarity and inspiration to live your life's purpose.

When you are in deep, dreamless sleep, your mind is offline. Although you are not alert via your senses, the subtle pranic field is still operating because you continue to breathe and stay alive. Refocusing your attention on these refined layers during your meditation practice, for example, can help facilitate a more profound meditative experience.

There is always energy available to us that resides in the universal consciousness. With this awareness, we can make decisions wisely, with clarity and precision, and without the ego and personal thoughts clouding them. We become conscious of the *Self*, not *self-conscious*, centered in the *Self*, not *self-centered*.

## CAUSAL BODY—THE SPIRIT AND SOUL

The next kosha, the causal body, is the realm of the spirit and soul, and gives rise to both our physical and subtle bodies. This layer of our being grants us access to information from our internal states of awareness, rather than from outside sources. Here, you will experience pure awareness. Very few meditators have done the practices to gain awareness of the causal body. The luminosity at this level is an experience, and through continued sustained practices the practitioner gains access.[8]

**What are the practices that can help seekers attain this level?**
In Yoga Science, there are three practices mentioned that are used to reach this level of awareness: selfless service, intensely focused meditation, and devotion to God. Ask yourself these questions: "Do you predominantly identify with your body?" Do you identify with power and vitality?" "Do you identify with an analytical mind?" "Do you most often identify with intuitive intelligence?"[9]

———————O———————

Our radiance and luminosity appear as we transcend these coverings of self-identification. Once we "take the lampshade off," we step in the light of our true Self. The quality of light is dependent upon the purity of our minds; the purity of mind is dependent upon our ability to focus. Our ability to focus is dependent upon our level of inner and outer balance.

In the next chapter, I will describe the chakras and show how they work to serve as centers of transformation.

# CHAPTER 6

———————○———————

# The Energy Centers

*All the healing forces found at our energy centers are available to us. We must access them in order to heal, nourish, and transform into our radiant selves.*

According to the philosophies of Yoga Science, wherever prominent energy currents meet or cross over, we have an energy field called a "chakra."

Our pranic or vital energy body is fueled by the chakras—subtle, high-powered vortices of energy in the body. They provide the foundation for our physical, emotional, mental, and spiritual well being. Each of the chakras is associated with one of the layers that we discussed in the last chapter. They receive and store the vital energy from the more subtle channels and act as transformers to deliver energy to our physical organs, as well as to our body mechanisms. In advanced states of consciousness, chakras act as "switches" to give us access to higher dimensions of conscious awareness and serve to bring us into radiance.

Although they are not physical, from a neurophysiological perspective chakras are associated with nerve plexuses in the spinal column. The location of each chakra is identified and associated with certain endocrine glands and internal organs. This is an oversimplification of the system. Instead, perhaps we should look at aligning the chakras with neural centers of the autonomic nervous system.

The full science of the chakras is beyond the scope of this book. However, I want to give you an overview of all of them before we focus on the three chakras that I refer to as *hubs of radiance*—the hara, head, and heart. The hara, head, and heart are fundamental to our *Return to Radiance* program. For a more detailed discussion, refer to our *Resilience Training Online Course*.[1]

The first chakra, known as the *Mūlādhāra Chakra*, is located in the area of the perineum in men, and the opening of the cervix in women. It is the generator of our vital energy. The second chakra, located at the base of the spine, is called the *Svādhiṣṭhāna Chakra*, and is related to the lumbar plexus, the female and male reproductive organs. The third chakra is associated with the solar plexus, adrenal glands, pancreas, and is the storehouse of our vital energy. It is located at the navel, or the hara. This is the *Maṇipūra Chakra*, known in Yoga Science as "the city of gems." In Western terms, it is referred to as the seat of our metabolic center. The fourth is the heart chakra, or *Anāhata Chakra*, and is the seat of consciousness. It is associated with the cardiac plexus, thymus gland, and pericardium. The fifth, or *Viśuddha Chakra*, is associated with the thyroid gland and is located at the level of the throat. The sixth, *Ājñā Chakra*, is known as the command center, the seat of the mind. It concentrates and directs our vital energy, and correlates with the pineal gland. Its entry point is located at the eyebrow center, and it is the point of confluence where the three main nadis, or forces—*Ida*, *Pingala* and *Sushumna*—merge into one stream of energy that moves up to the seventh chakra. The seventh chakra, *Sahasrāra*, is located at the crown of the head and is associated with universal consciousness.

While the chakras correspond to physical plexus throughout the body according to the Philosophy of Yoga Science and Taoism, they are also centers of energy—the life force, or *shakti*—our vitality.

The vital energy that gives us life is already awakened and is referred to as *prana*. There is also an abundance of untapped energy dormant within us—this is the shakti, or what is referred to as kundalini energy. This life force that is generated when our dormant energy awakens is contained in the cerebrospinal fluid. It travels upward through the inside of the spinal column, passing through the energy centers, or chakras, and moves along thousands of energy pathways.

For those aspirants who choose to study and practice, a source of unlimited energy awaits. The vast part of our brain awakens, and more resources become available to us. When our dormant energy awakens, our life becomes illuminated with radiance. There are many excellent books on the profound action and implications of the chakra system. Since the focus of this book is on vitality and rejuvenation, the program focuses on activating our powerful energy center associated with our third chakra—hara, which will lay the foundation for us to access the sixth—our head—where we concentrate our energy, and the fourth—our heart—where our "living mind" dwells. Yoga Science tells us that access to our health and vitality can be managed through these energy hubs. When these energy hubs are in complete balance, vitality flows through all seven chakras. You might wonder why we don't start at the first chakra, since it is the generator of our vital energy. The reason is that it is far easier to gain access to the third, fourth, and sixth chakras. Therefore, we start with the third chakra, or hara. When we work with this energy center we ignite our metabolic fire and improve our digestion, immunity, and confidence level. It is far more accessible than the first two chakras, and much easier to control. When we work with the sixth center between the two eyebrows, we gain command over the pranic energy flow.

As we learn to concentrate on it, we can move the energy from our head and gain access to our heart. It is the foundation for any work in self-development and transformation. When we focus on our fourth center, the heart, compassion begins to unfold. Interesting fact: the Sanskrit word for mind is *chitta*, which also means heart; coincidentally chitta resides in the heart. The same word is used for heart and mind in several other Asian languages.

Creating a balance between the hara, head and heart is our path to radiance. These descriptions illustrate how the energy of the chakras serves as a doorway to the realm of our existence. As mentioned above, they are associated with the spinal column but are not confined in the body. These energy hubs extend beyond the boundaries of the physical body.

Here is a brief description of the hara, head, and heart chakra taken from Pandit Rajmani Tigunait, Ph.D, in his course, Living Tantra:

*Consciousness fills the space of our heart; it is the filling of the space that creates our entire physical manifestation—the manifestation of our body, brain and nervous system. Our energy currents move down from the heart, and a big powerful vortex which is created below the heart is called our solar plexus. The one above our heart is the eyebrow center. Each energy current corresponding to these different locations is infused with its own characteristics. Additionally, each center of these energy matrices has its own shakti or what is termed in the spiritual world, a deity, but in our health and medical science world it is known as energy and science.[2]*

We noted that energy travels from the first, the lowest chakra, to the highest chakra. Think of our energy system as an ascending staircase of a building, stopping off at each floor. On each floor we find different offices with varying activities. Unimpeded energy can move freely up the staircase, but detours or blocks can trap the energy in one of the "offices," and then it does not fully or effectively ascend to the higher levels, or floors. As noted, *when shakti energy travels in the body, there may be impediments.* This is why we have practices that help to move our energy through the different levels until we reach states of higher realization or awareness. Proper diet, nutrition, and movement, breathing, and thought processes will ensure that these energy centers function optimally.

Ultimately, our goal is to work through the psychological and spiritual issues that we have in each of our energy centers and resolve them. When we are free from these issues and able to avoid stagnation in our life, we can enjoy the pleasures of the world and still be free to achieve a full spiritual life.

———O———

I spoke earlier of *prana*, or *shakti*, the life force that is the essence of all living things. As long as we continue breathing the process of manufacturing energy will continue. Breathing is the vehicle that carries prana along; it is the key to life. If it stops, our bodies die. Breath connects the consciousness of both mind and body; it brings energy to our cells through our nerves, veins, and arteries (our nadis), those branches that keep our metabolic functions running.

The breathing process itself is a neuromotor action; inhalation and exhalation are performed with the help of the nervous system. When we are in the womb, the pranic force flows to us from the lungs of our mother through the umbilical cord located at our navel center. When we enter the world, our own lungs take over, but the *hara* center remains key to our prana, for it is the center of our digestion and is the origin of the pranic channels—the nadis. The *hara* center, the seat of metabolism, energizes and empowers all other systems of the body; its chakra is associated with fire both physically and metaphorically. Patently, the hara center is vital in maintaining our willpower and transforming will into action. It provides the energy we need to move forward and achieve our destiny. This is why the *Return to Radiance* program is specifically designed to help you activate and cultivate energy at this center. The other two hubs, the head and heart, also become vital when we activate the third chakra, engage in breathing practices, and practice systematic meditation. I will get into the specifics of breathing and meditation techniques later. For now, let's focus on the fact that all the cells in our body move in harmony when our breathing is balanced. Breathing purifies the autonomic nervous system and gives vitality to the chakra centers of the body. If you learn to regulate your breath, you will not only maintain your energy, but you will bring a fresh source of energy to your entire life. Indeed, you will be able to "feel" the energy from the breath as it permeates your physical body as well as your subtle body. Sustained energy and alertness is not possible without controlled breathing; it conditions your physical, emotional, and mental aspects, and gives you access to the spiritual realm of life.

We saw earlier that the assimilation of nutrients and the elimination of toxins is determined by our digestive capacity. Western nutritionists look mainly at the physical components of food—fats, proteins, carbohydrates—and try to compose a properly balanced diet among them. Integrative practitioners specializing in nutrition pay attention to the physical components of food, as well as the way the food is grown, harvested, and handled. This shows them how much pranic energy is contained in the food. Integrative practitioners look at how diet and nutrition can feed our energy systems physically, emotionally, mentally, as well as spiritually.

The *Radiance Diet* offers guidance on all of the above and also addresses the three hubs of energy and their attendant chakras, which are essential to the mind's metabolism as well as the body.

———○———

All the healing forces found at our energy centers are available to us. We must access them in order to heal, nourish, and transform into our radiant selves. Those of us who have not gained access to these forces will be subject to the normal processes of aging and increased susceptibility to a variety of diseases.

You can assess your vitality in terms of the fire element that governs the third chakra. If it is balanced, you will feel energetic and assertive, but not aggressive. You will feel confident and passionate; your moods will be stable and your energy level will be sustained. However, if you are out of balance, you will feel anxious, lethargic, and either overly passive or overly aggressive. You will be quick to anger, quick to cry, and indigestion will be a frequent issue. By balancing your third chakra (hara), you will regulate the first two chakras as well, and generate the energy needed to sustain a focused mind and open heart.

If you are tired, you will lose energy quickly when you exercise, experience shortness of breath, get easily depleted and run down, or crave stimulants such as coffee and sweets. If this happens, you should pay attention to your hara (naval center). Without the right support and fuel for your body, you will see these patterns of depletion emerge.

The Science of Ayurveda views these symptoms as depleted vitality, or what is referred to as loss of *Ojas*. Ojas is the vital essence that supports energy and gives fuel for the mental, emotional, and metabolic fire to burn efficiently. To begin restoring vitality, you need to adjust your diet, sleep schedule, exercise routine and breathing patterns; this will regulate your metabolism. When our metabolism is strong, we glow with vitality, with life. We exude radiance.

————O————

As we grow older, our physical and psychological states change, as do our needs. When our physical state changes, the way we eat must change as well to accommodate our metabolic needs. Eating fresh, live food, non-polluted, and non-GMO (genetically modified organisms) is the first step toward establishing a healthy environment for our foundation. For most of us, it is impossible to eat farm-fresh food daily; at the very least we should be conscious of what we do consume. We need to try as much as possible to avoid the processed foods, canned foods, and refined sugars that sap the vitality from the nutrients, and in turn, from ourselves.

Food comes in a vast array of forms and produces various vibrational levels and types of energy in our bodies. As food is digested and processed chemically by the body, it supports the organ systems associated with each chakra. The *Radiance Diet* works to ensure that each organ system functions optimally. You might find it fascinating to note how closely foods and their psychological and physiological effects are related to our individual chakras. (Diagram on following page.)

| CHAKRA | 1 | 2 | 3 | 4 | 5 | 6 |
|---|---|---|---|---|---|---|
| **Physical Function** | elimination of solid waste, stability, groundedness | elimination of liquid waste, fluidity | digestion, assimilation, acid/alkaline balance, burning fuel | nurture, breathing, circulation, immunity, elimination | swallowing, expression, eliminating poisons, receiving | rectifies faults in other centers |
| **Psychological Function** | fearlessness | sexuality | willpower | love/compassion | ingenuity | imagination |
| **Associated Symptoms** | colds, tight hamstrings, paranoia | cystitis, low-back pain vaginitis, jealousy | digestive problems, sugar metabolism disorders, anger, inferiority | circulatory disorders, cancer, immune disorders, selfishness, overly emotional | sore throat, eating disorders, stubborn, pessimistic | headache, overthinking |
| **Foods for optimum function** | legumes, root vegetables, nuts and seeds | all fresh juices, liquids | complex carbohydrates | green leafy vegetables | fruits | herbs, working with the mind |

6.1 ILLUSTRATION - CHAKRA CHART

From this list, you can readily see which foods will specifically aid your energy and vitality. Our energy field must be tended to nutritionally. However, a food's value is more than just the physical components of carbohydrates, fats and proteins. Indeed, if food is fresh and alive, its vibrational energy will transcend the physical to affect all five senses, the brain, the mind, and even our soul.

———◯———

Just as there are specific foods that influence the individual chakras, there are also specific exercises. The exercises that are demonstrated later in the book address all energy centers, with focus specifically on the hara, head, and heart. Keep in mind that the exercises attend the physical, emotional, and mental components of our being.

Working with the body truly teaches you about your energy centers, revealing deep insight about yourself. Whenever there is an emotion around a powerful issue, or a sickness, the energy in the corresponding part of your body will be blocked. An interesting training for you to undertake is to observe what parts of your body experience the most challenges. Pay attention to your discomfort, and see what types of feelings and emotions arise. Keep in mind that we store a lot of tension in our abdomen and lower back that leads to stiffness and fatigue. Movement is the key to creating balance and opening the energy centers throughout your entire body.

Before giving a few suggestions on how to balance the vital energy currents, it is important to first know the principles of energy flow.

### Principles of Energy Flow

* Energy needs space to move.
* Movement of energy can be enhanced with cleansing.
* Energy needs a strong and flexible structure in which to move.
* Properly directed energy can be used to rejuvenate our entire being.

With these in mind, here are a few suggestions for balancing and optimizing your vital energy flow:

* Eat your "emotional foods" and the bulk of your calories between 10 a.m. and 2 p.m. This is when your body can digest food most efficiently, reserving more nutrients for your use.

* Follow the overnight diet as described in *Feeling Good Matters: The Yoga of Mind, Medicine and Healing.*[3] This gives your digestive system time to rest so that your body can do its housecleaning and get ready for the next day.

* Include high quality, well-prepared fresh foods in at least one meal daily. These foods give the cells of your body nutrients you need for the highest potential energy.

* Include thirty minutes of movement and exercise into your daily routine. This helps your energy to flow and return to balance.

* Include at least twenty minutes of relaxation and meditation time daily. This allows the body and mind time for rejuvenation.

———————O———————

Now that you have learned about energy centers, it is time to turn to the rest of the picture and observe the interaction between the mind and body.

# CHAPTER 7

───────○───────

# Mind-Body Response

*Nourishing the mind with joy, happiness, compassion, and love
through our associations and actions provides the
proper "diet" for our mind.*

Every time Jenny thinks about money, her lower back tenses and she experiences fatigue. When Beth is angry with her boss and keeps her thoughts inside, her skin begins to itch. Anne's fear of her economic security feeds her anxiety.

By now it's no secret that the body and mind are closely linked. Nowhere is this more evident than when it comes to the way we feed our mind and body—how and what we eat, and what we think. Indeed, our body is the manifestation of our thoughts. Anxiety often manifests itself in the neck, shoulders, and pelvis. If you're upset, your stomach secretes acid; when you are afraid, there's a rush of adrenaline. Claudia, one of my clients, developed asthma.

We were able to get to the root of it, only after she described how unhappy she was that her mother had moved into a nursing home. Sadness or grief often manifest in the lungs.

Take love, for example. To *experience* love we first need to love ourselves; we also need to keep our minds focused on our hearts. We must learn to clear away the fear, sadness, anger, jealousy, and frustrations that we may be unconsciously storing.

The practices of remaining calm and living in the moment allows us to collect, contain, and concentrate our energy. This trains the energy of the mind to stay concentrated and one-pointed. The overall benefit is the restoration or preservation of our energy. When we jump from thought to thought, we drain our energy, and vitality washes away. Diversions and distractions are experienced in the mind, but feelings first originate from the heart and then are transmitted to the body. Our diversions, distractions, and feelings can potentially lead to fatigue, overeating, or eating the wrong foods.

My friend, Sara, told me that every time she had to see her family, she would become agitated and anxious.

"All my mother has to say is 'hello' and I take a defensive stance," Sara said.

It became so overwhelming that she eventually avoided seeing her family.

Unfortunately when we are caught up in the past, it matters not whether our present thoughts are based on reality. When we hold onto our perceived ideas and don't look at each moment as it truthfully presents itself, we will get caught up in our old habit patterns. Sara could not free her mind enough to get beyond her past encounters with her family. That familiar old groove, thinking, or behavior pattern (known in yoga as a *samskara)* kept resurfacing every time she came in contact with her family. If Sara wants to change her perception of "what is," and not what was, she needs to visualize the change she wants to make, and then take the action to create it. The same is true for all of us who cling to our own unhealthy, habitual patterns of the past. Once we institute the change in ourselves, we will be more immune to the patterned behaviors of others; their actions will be of little or no consequence to us. We will have developed our own equanimity.

We need to be aware of the associations, thoughts, and impressions we experience, whether it's the food that we eat or the company we keep. Nourishing the mind with joy, happiness, compassion, and love through our associations and actions provides the proper "diet" for our mind. If we feed it daily with fear-filled aggressive thoughts, our mind will suffer. Just know that the mind feeds on all of the sensory impressions we offer it.

Freeing our minds from judgement and not taking others' actions personally are two practices we need to undertake if we want to cultivate joy and happiness in our lives. Eastern philosophers speak of the "one-pointed mind," and Tantric teachings explain that masters can remove the focus of their minds from their environments. It is often the unconscious mind, though, that prevents us from experiencing total freedom. We feel bound by our guilt, our regrets, our secrets, the teachings of society, our parents, and our early life programming.

There is no one more uninhibited than a young child. They are proud to be alive, walk with a strut, unashamed of nakedness, proud of their body and unchecked in mind. How quickly that freedom vanishes for many a youth as they move from the cradle to pre-school stage. "Don't do that!" "No!" "Put your clothes on!" "That is NOT nice." "Say you're sorry," "Say please," "Thank you," and on and on…the list of prohibitions tally up quickly in some families. By the time we reach school age, we are subjected to a new roster of rules and regulations that can smother our natural curiosity and interrupt our free flow of energy. Some of these "codes of conduct" may be adopted as absolute truth. Many of the beliefs and perceptions that we hold onto as truths keep us from experiencing all that life has to offer. By the time we become adults, we often have to unlearn much of what we were taught in the first 20+ years of our lives. A good number of us have developed habits that often deplete rather than replete us; however, it is never too late to change our habits.

Challenges in our upbringing, societal rules, and expectations aren't the only situations that can inhibit our thinking. Experiencing a traumatic event can have a lasting effect on our health and well-being. For example, if we have a sudden loss, we may experience a period where we are fully fatigued as well as depressed. If we can learn to acknowledge the feelings that arise, find compassion for ourselves and move forward, healing can prove to be uplifting. These traumatic situations are likely more debilitating for children, than if they are experienced in adulthood. In our *Resilience and Leadership* training, I emphasize that perception is the key to determining when and how quickly we will bounce back after a disturbing incident.

We start by becoming acquainted with our mind. Each of us

is part of a great universe, if we learn to recognize that we are all formed from the same elements of this earth, and the same energy, then we can see that there is no separation between you and me. With this realization, our mind field will flow freely. There will be no resistance that can weigh us down and exhaust us.

The vast reservoir of universal energy and our intrinsic state of brilliance is one and the same.

Meditation is one way to learn to work with our mind, and breath practice is the prerequisite to meditation. In truth, breath is the link between body and mind. As humans, we tend to create distinctions between ourselves and others. In reality, we are all the same. In Yoga Science, contemplation and meditation practices help us to overcome our feelings of separateness and teach us how to expand our awareness.

———————O———————

As we have mentioned, the ancient Yoga tradition tells us we are encased in five sheaths—the body, energy, and three dimensions of the mind (see chapter five). We have already discussed that through breath we can fathom the subtleties of the body sheath and the pranic (energy) sheath; we can also do this with the mind.

When we modulate the breath, we gain access to the patterns of our mind. In fact, the rhythm of the breath is the most obvious physical indication of a person's emotional or mental health. It is possible to determine a person's state of mind by listening to the rhythm of their breath. The strength of your breathing relates to everything you think or do. The less you fully use your lungs, the weaker your physical strength becomes; this adversely affects your entire metabolism. We have seen that rapid, shallow-chest breathing is synonymous with acute states of anxiety. Sometimes sighing (pausing after exhalation) indicates that a person is depressed. When we are angry or about to cry, we tend to hold our breath at the top of our inhalation. When we hold our breath without recognizing that we are doing so, our emotions become unsteady. Therefore, it is important to regulate our breath to support calmness and stability of body, mind, and spirit.

The body is the physical manifestation of the mind. When we change our thoughts, our body responds. Thoughts can be changed by changing breathing patterns, because modulating breathing patterns can heighten concentration. Breathing is something most of us do without any awareness of it. However, breathing is the one function of the nervous system that we can control thanks to the somatic nervous system. In other words, breathing happens whether we make an effort or not. However, if we so choose, we can regulate it with our mind. You may be aware of your own breath now because you are reading this book. When you are at work or in the middle of watching a movie, though, your focus is not on your breath unless you make a conscious effort to do so. I am not saying that you can be conscious of your breath all of the time; however, paying attention to your breath as often as possible will help you to remain calm. I am suggesting that through conscious breathing you can begin to change many physical and emotional aspects of yourself.

Again, breath and mind are intimately connected. Left-nostril dominance is associated with right-brain activities; right-nostril dominance is associated with left-brain activities. When you experience jerks in the flow of breath it indicates jerkiness in your thought process; the mind hops distractedly from one thought to another. Breathing irregularities express interruptions in your stream of thought. Pauses in your breath will intensify emotional states and shallow breathing de-energizes both body and mind, thereby numbing your awareness. In summary, if you are conscious of your breath you can change your physical, mental, emotional, and spiritual states.

To learn how to be conscious of your breath, start by becoming aware of the flow of breath through your nostrils. This allows you to have awareness of both your inner and outer environments, also known as the mind-body connection. Is your left nostril more active than your right, or vice versa? Every 90 to 120 minutes the nostrils switch dominance, but overall one nostril will be dominant most of the time (this varies from person to person). For example, suppose your left nostril is most active, and you decide to exercise. Chances are that the right nostril will dominate within a few minutes.

You can feel your nostrils switch with this simple practice. Breathe through each nostril, alternating as you hold the other one closed. Sense which nostril is more open. If you find it is the left, and you want to change your nostril dominance (which I don't recommend unless you have an underlying issue), lie down on your left side and pay attention to the right nostril. It will automatically become active within 10 minutes.

Ideally if you are balanced, your right nostril is dominant and open when:

You are physically active.

Your body is warm.

You are hungry.

You are eating.

You are engaging in short-term intense effort.

And you left nostril is dominant and open when:

You are quiet, at rest.

Your body is cool.

You are thirsty.

You are drinking liquids.

You are engaging in long-term sustained effort.

It is said that for optimal digestion, it is better to have the right nostril more dominant. For drinking liquids, the left nostril should be more active.[1]

During the practice of meditation when a person attains an advanced level of functioning, both nostrils flow equally. The central channel (Sushumna) is open and energy is free to rise and travel to the highest energy centers. We do get a glimpse of this when nostrils change dominance every ninety minutes or so, however it lasts less than a second. When you train your mind, you will learn how to hold that space where both nostrils are flowing equally for longer periods. This constitutes a deeper and more profound meditation practice.

If you pay attention to your breathing patterns, you'll be amazed at how quickly you become aware of when your mind and emotions come into play. With this awareness, you'll be able to pay attention to your immediate environment, and learn how to be free of distractions, fears and imaginations. You will experience more joy and tranquility.

————○————

Another function of breathing, via inhaling, is the ability to smell. Smelling the natural essences of flowers and herbs is transformative; whereas artificial perfumes and scents are actually disturbing to the mind. The sense of smell varies from person to person; what smells good to one individual may not be so great to another. The nose, through its terminal, the brain, is capable of distinguishing among thousands of specific smells. Remember, the limbic system is the seat of our emotions, and our olfactory bulbs—the organs responsible for smell—are connected to it. This is why smells can elicit such emotional responses. Along with touch, smell is our most primitive sense (it is the dominant one in many mammals). Our sense of smell is loaded with instinctive associations for all of us, which we can assume originated millions of years ago.

The relationship between the mind and smell has been recognized for millennia. Aromatic herbs and oils have been used as mood enhancers, aphrodisiacs, and seasoning for food since the earliest civilizations. *Kyphi*, an ancient Egyptian perfume, was thought to infuse sleep with bright dreams. The Greeks used aromatic oils as antidepressants, as sleep aids, and as aphrodisiacs. Today, researchers have found that smells can and do influence mood, evoke emotions, and counteract stress.[2] Products ranging from bathroom tissues to underarm deodorants are scented. I often wonder why some people saturate themselves with perfumes and colognes. Many of us end up experiencing headaches when we interact with manufactured scents; the mind-brain interface simply cannot handle the onslaught of chemical insults. When this occurs, I find it best to inhale a natural scent to counteract the artificial ones.

Fragrances can have a deep impact on our emotions. The cosmetic industry primarily depends on the use of artificial fragrances in their facial and body products to make them appeal to customers. Similarly, natural product companies provide fragrances and oils from natural sources in their products to calm and uplift the spirit. In this book's appendices, you will find a list of essential oils with some of their characteristics described.

As I have mentioned, smells have the power to unlock emotions. For instance, the scent of a flower can raise your spirits; the aroma of food can stimulate your appetite. Out of our five senses, the sense of smell has the greatest ability to awaken memories from our past.

Scents can affect our ability to concentrate, make us feel euphoric, calm us down, or stimulate and arouse us. When we bathe or massage with essential oils, we absorb some of their chemical constituents. I find that using oils of neroli, sandalwood, or frankincense, in a base of argon and sea buckthorn oil, are relaxing and leave my skin feeling nourished. Frankincense, especially, clears the air for meditation.

————O————

Food affects the mind as well as the body, which we have discussed and will see in more depth later. In the Ayurvedic system of nutrition, there are three types of foods based on three main *Gunas,* energetic qualities. These qualities have different effects on the mind and body.

## Tamasic Food

These foods tend to dull the mind, produce inertia, bring about what I call a "mental stupor," and are generally hard to digest. Processed meats, fats, most cheeses, fried foods, heavy sweets, cooked beef, chicken, and fowl all fall into this category.

## Rajasic Foods

These foods produce energy, speed up the metabolism, and stimulate the mind. They include pepper, ginger, hot spices, onions, coffee, canned foods, sweetened fruits, and fruit juices. Taken in moderation, rajasic foods will aid digestion as well as the mind. Overuse them and you will find yourself running at too fast a speed and becoming irritable and angry.

## Sattvic Food

These foods produce clarity, harmony and balance in the mind. Almost all vegetables and fruits are in this category, including artichokes, asparagus, dates, ghee, berries and figs. Honey is also a sattvic food.

The diets of most people include all three of these categories. In my experience, when we eat predominantly *well-prepared* sattvic foods, we are clearer and calmer than when we eat foods from the other two categories. Many people are not aware of the impact that diet and nutrition have on the mind. When working with your diet the point is to accept yourself; be neither too lax, nor too austere in your dietary practices. There's no question, though, that at some events a piece of chocolate cake is preferable to a philosophical discussion on Nietzsche. All rhubarb and no ginger makes Jill a dull woman.

Just as food can influence the mind, the mind can influence what foods we eat. At one of my recent lectures, I was talking about the benefits of the overnight diet. A woman raised her hand.

"What should I do when I want something crunchy and munchy at 11 p.m.?" She asked. Her tone and manner displayed edginess; her intense body language showed that my response was important to her.

"What's your normal diet?" I asked.

"A little meat and a lot of salad."

"Cookies? Candies? Potato chips?"

"No way. I need to stay thin."

"And, why do you want to stay thin?"

Her voice became defiant. "I have my reasons."

"I am wondering why you seem agitated and angry when I asked the question?"

Her face turned red and she gave a gasp, as though I had uncovered some secret. She quickly sat down. My intention was certainly not to expose her inner discomfort. Although, this situation did give me an opportunity to explore the issues around food and the mind-body response to it.

"When we are angry or unsettled," I told the group, "we often crave crunchy foods, or maybe some ice cream. Because we sometimes try to fill our emptiness with food, eating momentarily satisfies those feelings. Similarly, when we are depressed, or feeling unworthy and unattractive, we crave sweet soft foods containing fats and carbohydrates—"comfort foods."

If you approach your diet from a personal and experiential point of view, it will reveal a lot about how your mind works and what your are feeling on a deeper level. The practices of eating on time, quality of food, and how much your need to fulfill your physical and mental needs will transform your understanding of nourishment.

I never had the opportunity to work privately with the woman from the lecture who was depriving herself of nourishment. Had I the opportunity, I would have suggested that she include at least one cooked meal per day. A warm, well-prepared meal does wonders for the mind and creates the sustaining feeling of nurturance for your entire being. I would have suggested she keep her salad, but only as a side dish. I would also have her add supplements to her diet, including herbs, that would be nourishing and produce a sense of wholeness and contentment.

In *Ayurvedic Healing: A Comprehensive Guide*, Dr. David Frawley states:

*Emotions have the same effect (on our bodies) as foods or herbs of the same energetic quality. Anger can damage the liver as much as alcoholism. So herbs and diet are not enough if the taste of the mind has not changed.*[3]

Obviously the physical and emotional cravings we have for certain foods are strong. The answer to the simple query, "why don't we change our diet and eat wholesome foods," is because it is not so easy.

————○————

From a biochemical perspective, our blood-sugar level is one of the biggest contributors to our moods; it factors heavily in relationship to our level of fatigue and depression.

When we have a steady supply of glucose in our bloodstream, we don't experience radical shifts in mood or energy levels. Do you get moody at certain times of the day? If you do, it is most likely that you have had a drop in your blood-sugar level. A glass of diluted grape juice will balance things better than grabbing that 4 p.m. candy bar or eating a frozen yogurt. Eating oatmeal in the morning instead of sugary cereal is more stabilizing to your blood sugar. The sweetened cereal may cause your body to produce too much insulin, and as a result you will experience a quick drop in energy after eating. Oatmeal (with a fresh-fruit topping, if you want) takes longer to digest, and you will have a regulated flow of insulin during digestion. The result is that the glucose level stays constant, allowing your mind and body to stay alert. For some of us, depending on our age and biochemistry, a little protein would be a better choice for breakfast, along with a piece of fruit. I always go with the premise that "one diet does not fit all." If your diet is not working for you, it is always a good idea to consult with someone who is well-trained in nutrition to assist you with your questions or concerns.

————○————

All animals share the same primal urges for food, sleep, self-preservation, and sex. Humans, though, are the only creatures who have the ability to override nature and regulate these urges consciously. Our awareness and intelligence give us the privilege to become free to experience higher levels of consciousness. A Tantric master will transcend all the primitive urges to devote their physical, mental, and spiritual life to attain self-realization.

The vast majority of us, however, will be influenced and limited to some degree, by our primitive urges. The more we include the spiritual perspective when it comes to working with these urges, the closer we come to our radiance. All of our encounters produce an experience; the intention behind our thinking and actions determines the outcome.

Let's consider the fountain of sex. When we engage in sexual union, we exchange our energy with another human being with the potential for creating a new life. Either consciously or unconsciously, we're all aware of this. The instinctive desire to procreate is what drives attractions in the first place, even for women unable to conceive. This is our innate connection to the universal energy of creation.

When we lose passion for love, we tend to redirect our energy into other areas such as food, or sleep. We may become depressed or feel unworthy and we turn to comfort foods. When we are unhappy with our lives, we can turn to all sorts of distractions—food, sex, sleep, social media, etc. We create a barrier by insulating ourselves from other people. Let me give you an example.

Early on in my career when I first wrote the book *Sexual Radiance*,[4] I had a client, we will refer to her as Jessica. She came to me after ending a relationship that she originally thought would be the beginning of her married life. Jessica was an attractive and wise woman, but simply put, her "heart was broken," and that feeling had lead her to spiral down into old habit patterns. She started eating at night when she returned home after work. In the past, she would meet her lover and enjoy their evenings together. After the relationship ended, though, Jessica was eating round the clock. Her weight gain became the physical manifestation of what was going on in her mind. Jessica was filling the need to be loved with food. Once we talked about Jessica's feelings of not being loved, we were able to address her weight. At night, I had her substitute exercise for her nightly food habit, followed by a bath with essential oils. I also gave her a flower essence formula that worked with her mind and heart to help increase her self-confidence and eliminate her self-doubt. It took several months of continual work, but when she began to shed pounds, her confidence increased. Jessica was then able to observe herself more closely and understand why she had been over eating. This example illustrates that it is possible to change physical habits created by our mind if we become aware of their source.

---

Before we turn to the *Return to Radiance* program, I would like to mention two other issues related to food: binging and stress. I talked about cravings earlier, and how they often reflect our emotional needs. Binging also reflects our emotional state. When people binge they are unconsciously trying to fill the emptiness they feel inside. Once they have filled themselves physically, the inability to accept nourishment and love triggers a guilt response, they literally reject the food that is in their body.

Irene binged. She would starve herself throughout the day and eat all night. The trick she played on herself began with the two boxes of cookies she would eat on the way home from work. She always planned to start her diet "tomorrow." Over time, Irene found herself gaining weight. She became despondent and found herself doing less and less. She would often fall asleep on the couch after eating while watching a Netflix series. She came to me to uncover the real reason behind her weight gain.

To understand these problems, first and foremost, we have to deal with the biochemistry of it all. The body requires certain nutrients to sustain a balanced life. Based on my years of clinical work in diet and nutrition, I have learned that the first step is to get the physical digestion up and running. When the body's physical digestive process becomes balanced, the minds' ability to balance itself soon follows. Therefore, we first create a nutrition plan consisting of light, moist, and digestible foods in order for the body and mind to become settled.

Erratic dietary habits can cause stress on both the body and mind, and stress delivers a pretty good guarantee that the sufferer will end up fatigued. When this occurs, our lives just seem to be about existing, and not in a productive, happy way. When we are fatigued, we tend to fall back on our old ways of eating. We create a cycle. We create a cycle of poor diet choices, leading to fatigue, and the cycle repeats.

Stress has its origins in the mind. Like a cascading waterfall, our body experiences the brunt of the mental disturbance as it pools around us. Stress is the message our mind gives to our body that danger exists: if we are afraid we are going to be fired—we feel *stress*. If we are fatigued by lack of rest or over-thinking, our *stress response* is activated. If we are fatigued because of a poor diet choice, *food stress* is at fault. If we are too tired, come home late, and don't exercise there is *more stress*.

The true purpose of stress is to prepare the body for a survival response. While sometimes it is a great benefit (like when a car is heading straight at us and our adrenaline rises in response and we jump out of the way), the stress response conditioning has unfortunately become a way of life. Our worrying or overthinking minds send misleading or unnecessary messages to our bodies, and our adrenal glands react as if something is actually happening. Unlike animals who return to their normal rhythm after the threat is gone, we tend to hold on and not let it go. We ruminate on what was, what could have happened, or what we believe might still happen, long after the perceived threat has vanished. We stay in the stress response, and create long term harm to our organs. Let's say that you do indeed have something come up and you lose your job. If you have trained your mind to remain calm through meditation, you might look at the situation as an opportunity to expand your awareness and learn another skill. If you are able to be calm and centered in that moment, chances are stress is non-existent.

Meditation—as an exercise to train the mind—is a fine vehicle for becoming clear and one-pointed. Although people use it as a means for reducing stress which is one benefit, it is not the sole purpose of meditation. When all the senses are sealed and our minds become one-pointed, we can feel extreme joy and balance. Meditation is one of the greatest gifts that you can give to yourself; included in this book is an entire chapter on its purpose, function, and method.

The nature of life is constant change. It is up to us to practice maintaining our balance. Most of us will have ups and downs throughout the span of our life. My moods have fluctuated as my work and self-esteem have changed. The last four decades spent in meditation practice has afforded me a more stable life; I am able to step back and observe my mind and not get caught up in its imaginings. However, there are times where I find myself mired by old mental habits.

We have all been in situations where we are honored, loved, unloved, or dishonored. This is all part of the experience of life. What we must do to be vital and happy is learn to be unaffected by outside influences, recognize that we are radiant human beings, and step into our light. In my book, *Feeling Good Matters*, I discuss the teachings I received from a Yoga Master about how to live in the world and remain above. Understanding who we truly are and learning to live in equanimity allows us to enjoy what the world has to offer.

———○———

We have covered how the energy systems support the mind-body response. It is now time to turn specifically to the science of inner life, which ultimately reflects our radiance.

# CHAPTER 8

———————O———————

# The Science of Inner Life

*There is no question that to be radiant is to be vital—*
*indeed, radiance requires balanced*
*physical and mental energy.*

Tantra, the science of inner life, is a four-thousand-year-old discipline leading to physical, mental, and spiritual self-mastery. By bringing together all aspects of life, Tantra teaches essential practices that serve to illuminate our vitality, and show us the way to return to radiance.

Tantra literally means "a web," an interweaving of all aspects of the human condition—physical, psychological, emotional, and spiritual—where total freedom and fulfillment can be found. Tantra leads us to radiance—the inner luminosity which occurs when we are energetic and vital. My aim is to bring some aspect of this discipline to the West, but it is beyond the scope of this book to explain all the facets of Tantra. I will attempt to lift the veil on its association with sex since that is what most people in the West associate with the word *Tantra*.

Tantra is a discipline, and the mind often rebels against discipline. Our mind also tends to be drawn toward immediate gratification and pleasure from outside sources. It is easy to see how Tantra is misunderstood and veiled in ignorance, as its far reaching perspective is unfamiliar to many of us.

The purpose of Tantra is spiritual union, not physical and emotional gratification. A student of Tantra discovers that the aspects and things of the world are there for our use, not paths to follow. Perhaps a more accurate way to describe the principle here is to speak of Tantra as a gateway to inner discipline. This inner discipline is required in order to access our radiance.

Further, Tantra is a branch of Yoga Science that teaches the value and importance of experience in the transformation of our actions. The goal of Tantra is to seek inner awareness, selflessness, and enlightenment. Many schools of yoga seeking the same goals insist on monastic life—renunciation, detachment, and asceticism—but Tantra does not. The aim is to fully discover and realize each part of our daily life as a part of our spiritual practice, a vehicle to study ourselves and study life.

Pleasure and enjoyment are a part of life, yet seekers are cautioned not to become lost in sensual experiences. Yogic practices are used for self-inquiry, and ultimately, spiritual attainment and freedom. As we saw in the last chapter, if we are to have freedom and fulfillment, the body needs to be cleansed and nourished (through sound diet and breathing), and the mind must be calm and focused (through meditation). All of our energy flows as a river flows. Even if you are not familiar with energy concepts or don't believe in this philosophy, there is much to be learned and applied in our return to radiance.

Perhaps the element that I appreciate most is that in Tantra, women are honored and adored. The form of the Divine in Tantra is *She* who is the mother (the womb), and is therefore endowed with all creative aspects of life both positive and negative. As we've seen, the kundalini shakti—latent energy—resides within all of us just waiting to be awakened. When this energy remains dormant, we are only aware of earthly things and earthly functions. This is where we remain trapped in our habit patterns that do not support higher aspects of being human. However, with precise, skillful, and systematic practices, we can open our energy pathways and experience more of or hidden potential.

While many cultures still suppress women and do not give them reverence and respect, in Tantra the female aspect is celebrated, in some respects, worshipped. Many times I wonder what happened to the revered woman who had rights and positions of high esteem and did not have to protest for equality. Women are now waking up to address these questions. On the other end of the spectrum men are now being attacked for simply being male. Until balance is achieved with mutual respect and love, human beings cannot reach their greatest potential. Both woman and man are on a mutual journey to come together and blend their strengths and their finest qualities. Since we all have a desire for health and happiness, Tantra teaches us to let that desire lead the way toward growth on our way to enlightenment.

There is no question that to be radiant is to be vital—indeed, radiance requires balanced physical and mental energy. I have spent time with many sixty-year old women who are enthusiastic and naturally beautiful, and are living life with no regrets. I have learned their secret; they practice allowing only positive thoughts to flow. They have learned to avoid identifying with negative thoughts or impressions. Therefore, gossip is not on the menu. These women have a daily habit of meditation, they are not stressed, so their breathing is smooth and rhythmic. They bring their life into meditation. These women glow. Their energy is conserved, not dissipated by over-thinking, worrying, judging, or other habits that will pull them away from their pure, brilliant center of being. They tell me that they don't fear death; they are here to serve and be the best people that they can be. The energy of this type of mind is clear, tranquil and intentional. I have learned much from observing these souls who exude pure radiance.

A Tantric master I had the privilege of knowing, once said, "You are the architect of your life and you decide your destiny." He was talking about self-mastery—control over the physical, emotional, and spiritual aspects of our lives. As I move through life, this wisdom has been a guide for me. We are the sum total of our thoughts and actions. When we train our mind through the practices given to us by these masters, our life transforms.

The concept of self-mastery can seem scary to some when students first hear of it, especially now when people even struggle to find the time to prepare their own meals. I have heard some students say, "It seems so hard, I am not that interested." Self-mastery, put simply, requires self-knowledge, self-discipline, and systematic training, which can be achieved with right diet, proper breathing, and meditation. Our habits, built through our lifetime, often get in the way. I have studied with several Eastern masters and was struck by the fact that none of them seemed to age in a "normal" fashion. They were far more energetic than Westerners their age. Their skin looked younger; they had better posture, and they walked with more confidence. They had conscious control of their mind and it translated to their thinking. All of them followed a regimen of proper diet, meditation, and breathing to support a clear, tranquil, and one-pointed mind. They lived in the present, the NOW. I have adopted and simplified some aspects of their practices in my program for Westerners—specifically for the needs and benefit of Western women.

Self-knowledge, discipline and systematic training—let's look at them one at a time.

## SELF-KNOWLEDGE

A simple definition of self-knowledge is the ability to recognize what is useful to you and *what* is not, combined with the ability to understand *why* you act as you do and react as you do. By understanding what shapes your actions and the way your mind works, you can begin to recognize your unconscious habits. What you might have described previously as your "quirky" behavior will now have meaning and can be viewed with deeper understanding.

Lauren mentioned to me that she was experiencing incontinence issues periodically and was told by her physician it was normal with aging. She was a bit unhappy since she was only 50 years young! Her hormone levels were still within the normal range. I attempted to find a solution to her problem since I too had experienced this earlier in life. As a yoga therapist, I decided to recommend some breathing and movement practices to her. These practices are generally not available in a standard medical setting. I felt Lauren would benefit from one of the best tools for developing self-awareness, the alternate nostril breathing practice.

Right now, are you aware of whether your right or left nostril is dominant when you breathe? Take a moment to determine if it is your left or right side. Close off your right nostril with your thumb, and breathe through your left nostril. Then close off your left nostril with your ring finger, and breathe through your right nostril. Which nostril has the most air flowing through it? After this exercise, you may find yourself noticing the flow of your breath more often during the day. Through the practice of being mindful of your breath, you have become aware of something you do unconsciously, thousands of times during the day.

I asked Lauren to try alternate nostril breathing and explained that self-awareness is an essential step toward self-knowledge.

"Now, Lauren, pay attention to the alignment of your pelvis when you are experiencing incontinence, then bring your awareness to your breathing and notice how you feel. For example, is something going on unconsciously that you are bringing to the surface with your breath?"

"I was feeling tightness in my gut, Dr. Taylor, and I realized the issue that was coming up for me was fear."

"Were you feeling threatened at all?" I asked.

"Yes, I was ruminating over a family encounter."

"Let me guess, your body tensed, throwing off your pelvic alignment, and you wonder what your bladder was feeling?"

Lauren looked at me and smiled. "Wow," she said.

On her next visit, she happily shared her success.

"I was able to work with my pelvis just as you taught, and relax it by paying attention to my breath if it got tense. I am not 100% successful yet, but I am truly amazed by how I can relieve the tension, and I feel like walking is also easier. That's something that I have not felt in *years*."

I know from experience, that awareness of the physical aspects of our lives can lead us to an awareness of the way our mind works. Having taught this concept in healing retreats around the country, I tell participants, "Use your body as feedback." Why? Because the mind cannot analyze itself; however, the body is a direct reflection of what is going on emotionally and psychologically. Remember, the mind and body are intrinsically connected.

One good method for developing self-knowledge through self-awareness is to keep a journal for any insights you may have. The habit of journaling supports the process of self-enquiry. Self-enquiry, also spelled, self-inquiry, is the constant attention to the inner awareness of "I," or "I am." This practice was recommended by Master Sri Ramana Maharshi as the most efficient and direct way to discover who you are beyond the labels that you use to identify yourself.

Awareness is about paying attention and is an important part of acquiring self-knowledge. Since gaining knowledge relies on observing ourselves, our ability to be aware of our inner self is only as good as the observations that have been made. Journaling supports this process.

I have worked with many clients that have recognized the subtle cause of their illness by gaining awareness and access to their thoughts and emotions. Emma, one of my clients, had consistent migraines. I recommended that she keep a daily written log of her food intake, as well as her feelings and emotions. I asked her to correlate this with her headaches—what had she eaten and what had she been feeling a day or two before her headaches occurred? Very soon the answer revealed itself—dairy foods in combination with chicken meals. These were her go to foods when she felt stressed. We recognized that her digestive power was diminished from the stress of her job; on top of that, she was dampening her digestive fire by eating heavy, dense, and hard-to-digest foods. Once she removed those foods from her diet, her headaches disappeared. In order to deal with her stress, a different dietary protocol was required.

Many people feed their stress with poor food choices; soon the mental dilemma becomes a physical problem. Awareness of what you eat and how you eat in relation to your moods builds self-knowledge. Ask yourself this: after you eat sugar, do you feel depressed or anxious? Do you crave chips when you are angry? Do you get sleepy after meals? If you can recognize your physiological state, you can also interpret your psychological one. If you learn to recognize the interplay of your feelings, thoughts, habits, and actions, you will be able to transform self-destructive behavior—whether it be physical or mental—into those behaviors that are good for your body, mind, and your soul.

## SELF-DISCIPLINE

The word "Discipline" sounds punitive, like a type of punishment, especially to the Western mind. However, when combined with willpower, discipline becomes the second factor in self-mastery. It is a positive—indeed, essential element—in a full, more realized, vital life. No long-lasting life change is possible without discipline. Sometimes, of course, discipline *does* feel like punishment. Recently, a client who adores ice cream told me, "I've cut out sweets entirely."

"Good for you," I said, eyeing her dubiously. "Do you feel better for it?"

"Better?" She cried. "It's torture!"

Precisely. Discipline does not mean adherence to a regimen that will "do you good." And it does not correlate with being driven. What it does mean, though, is the application of willpower to point you toward a desired goal. *Willpower* means mind-strength. *Discipline*, its sister, means the ability to apply that strength when needed. When it comes to dieting, for instance, start simply; cut down without cutting out. When it comes to exercise, work with the concepts of stability and comfort in mind. When it comes to meditation, start with five minutes, not an hour. The mind can be very resistant to change, especially if one's habits are deeply embedded. Discipline is not about pain, it is gently massaging your mind so that you can accomplish your best intentions and experience fulfillment.

Remember, discipline is a mental practice which ultimately manifests in the physical. A positive mindset is a prerequisite. The word *"can't"* creates an obstacle in the mind that reinforces defeat. "I want to do it. I can do it. I will do it." These are the words I heard from a Yoga Master. Remembering these words will take you a long way toward achievement. It takes discipline to think positively, but the rewards are many.

## SYSTEMATIC TRAINING

What is systematic training? As an adjunct of discipline, systematic training simply means that you need to employ an organized, regular sequence in your exercise and meditation time. You must be able to do both within your capacity, while being flexible enough to make adjustments from time-to-time, depending on external influences. For example, this could mean having a brief relaxation before meditation. In order to be successful in systematic training, you must set the intention and make a commitment to yourself that is consistent with your lifestyle, and follow a precise and skillful program that has qualities you enjoy. You must also commit to do no harm to yourself, physically or psychologically.

In the *Return to Radiance* program, I ask women to chart their current schedules to find the optimum times for meditating, eating, and exercise. Changing their schedule often means they need to work with themselves to give up decades of old habits (eating lunch on the run, exercising only on weekends and meditating when there's time), and then create new habits. This program starts slowly, fifteen minutes for breathing and exercise, and five minutes for meditation. The cultivation of new habits is the benefit of systematic training—and habits can either be the greatest obstacle to self-mastery, or the greatest tool to achieve it.

————————○————————

If you accept modern psychology's premise that our behaviors are conditioned by seeking pleasure and avoiding pain, you can see that habits are created from developing a pattern of behavior. We come to regard our habits as a natural part of us; we usually don't consider the possibility of changing them.

Take diet, for example. When I ask my clients who are interested in weight reduction and anxiety reduction, to list what they eat, their answers are varied, although the messages are the same:

"I don't eat much."

"I try to stay away from sweets."

"I try to stay away from gluten."

"I stay away from fats."

"I eat a lot of vegetables."

These people are not consciously lying, yet their diet lists do not reflect what they are really doing. Many of them are not aware of what a measurement of "much" really means, nor do they actually know how far they "stay away" from sweets or fatty foods. They may not even be aware of what they're eating "a lot of", along with their vegetable consumption. When we analyze their food journals and I point out to them what they're *actually* eating, only then do they become aware of how ingrained their food habits have become. Many clients are astonished, and then they realize they need to make changes. What they must do first, of course, is to become self-aware. People get so used to their habits they don't see them clearly anymore. Developing self-mastery helps to restore their awareness.

When we correct habits that dull our awareness and blunt our alertness, we bring wonderful changes to our state of mind, metabolism, and health. When we're sick, we tend to regress psychologically and fall into old comfortable habits to protect ourselves. When we've regressed, we can't relate to others. When we are unable to relate, we're incapable of feeling energetic and vital—we lose radiance.

During old age or dangerous illness, our primitive habits can be protective and valuable. However, if we mistreat ourselves when we're young and we don't work to build different healthful habits, we'll never discover our true vitality.

————O————

There are five steps to creating useful habits:

1.  *Recognize* that you need to change.

    If you begin a self-awareness journal, you'll quickly be able to see what habits have brought you where you are today. Your *awareness* will be expanded. You can more easily take a look and see if your habits have created obstacles that block what you really want in your life.

2.  *Identify* the habit that you want to create.

    In your journal, write down your goal and the steps to reach the goal. If the goal is energy and vitality, one habit you may consider is the overnight fast (chapter nine). If you want to establish a habit of meditation, I tell students to create the intention to sit in the same space at the same time for five minutes each day.

3. Be *systematic*.

Make sure that you practice your new chosen habit at the same time each day. If you want to add alternate nostril breathing to your day, pick an optimum time to do it, and commit to it for at least twenty-one days. You will find that over the course of a month, you will have established a solid routine, and you won't want to miss your daily practice.

If you find that you are having problems, remember Step 5!

4. Be *consistent and persistent*.

It takes anywhere from twenty-one to forty days to create a new habit, so for the first month or so you'll have to be conscientious and maintain your schedule. I once worked with a woman named Carrie, who had trouble relaxing. She would get up and have coffee first thing in the morning, before doing her meditation. She did this for many years. It took tremendous discipline for her to switch to warm water with lemon in the morning before her practice, followed by her coffee routine between 9 a.m. and 10 a.m. Now though, she tells me that her mind is calmer and her meditation is more enjoyable.

5. Be *flexible*.

The ability to make adjustments when needed will help you stay with your routine. Therefore, if the time of day, the kind of beverage, or the strenuousness of the exercise becomes a burden, be flexible. If you become too rigid with rules and regulations, tension builds. If you over-tighten a guitar string, it will break; if you are too rigid with yourself, your good intentions will break. You should enjoy yourself! Useful habits should bring joy not only in their lasting effects, but also in the practices themselves.

————○————

Does all that apply when we return to radiance? Absolutely. Self-mastery is an essential part of having energy and vitality, as are its components.

Our daily life can benefit from a routine, even when our duties seem more like a chore. When we feel dissatisfied with our lives, it is not uncommon for our untrained minds to create fantasies. The problem is that the fantasy mind becomes an obstacle to achieving greater awareness. We must learn to step beyond the mind's tendency to crave pleasures and sensation; meditation and its practices will teach us how. This does not mean you cannot enjoy the pleasures of the world; instead focus on enjoyment without the dependency. True joy and inner happiness ultimately comes from love—self-love first, then loving others transpires spontaneously. When we have love in our lives, we can embrace our duties with enthusiasm. Love sustains itself because of this simple truth: service to others without expectation yields happiness. Once we get a glimpse of this, the beauty within ourselves and outside of ourselves cannot be hidden. The veil of fatigue, frustration, and fearful thinking is lifted. This is the moment we *return to radiance*.

True radiance, though, can be achieved if you are committed to being healthy and following a plan that incorporates a clean diet, balanced breathing, and fluid movement. This practice will create mind-breath-body synergy. These fundamental steps will move you in the direction that best serve you and ultimately guide you to self-mastery. Mastery of inner life requires that a person:

- Regulate their food intake with right time, right quality, and right quantity.
- Eat foods that support metabolism, not overload it.
- Fast at night to make sure the body and mind can do their metabolic work unimpeded.

When we develop self-mastery, we are able to control our habits of taste. Self-mastery requires that we regulate our urges so that our physical being is in union with our soul. Remember, mastery puts you in charge.

Masters of inner life are in control of their breath. They know that they have the power to bring their entire autonomic nervous system into balance by controlling their breathing pattern. They have discovered the subtle aspects of their breath that provide energy and nourishment to their mind and body.

As I have referenced before, the Tantric masters know the mind and body are one. Our bodies have the capacity to hold emotions. When these emotions are negative, blockages can form. Psychological stress—often unconsciously experienced—may lead to stiffness in the back or shoulders; anxiety will disturb the heart rate and close down the chest; anger will cause the liver to overheat creating many metabolic consequences; fear will cause the sacrum and pelvis to tighten.

Movement is an important means of unlocking old emotions. Once released and brought into your awareness, these emotions can be acknowledged and dealt with. When I work with women, I find that they sometimes become overwhelmed during yoga asana practice when releasing deeply held emotions. This is not an uncommon phenomenon. Great therapists like Ilana Rubenfeld can bring out repressed emotions by manipulating the feet, backs, or other areas of their patients' bodies. So exercise—intentional movement—will lead to a healthier body as well as a healthier mind.

Exploring inner life requires clearing the mind and body of all the obstacles that get in the way of our joy and prosperity. To be radiant requires that our body, mind and spirit are integrated so our energy can flow freely.

The Tantric master is a person who has mastered all aspects of the mental and spiritual self as well as her physical being. We do not have to become Tantric masters, though to adopt Tantric principles and embrace our radiance. We can begin the journey of self-mastery with the basic tenets of right diet, movement, breathing, and the preparation for meditation.

As you move forward, remember to seek relationships with those who are on the same journey, otherwise the path will be difficult to follow. The goal is to walk the path so each one of us can step into light.

———————○———————

I have covered the biochemical and philosophical ingredients for energy and vitality. Now we will turn specifically to the elements mentioned above to make it happen—diet, breathing, exercise and meditation.

PART III

A Total Program
for Radiance

# CHAPTER 9

―――――○―――――

# The Radiance Diet

*The Radiance Diet will allow you to derive maximum*
*benefits from the foods you eat, with the most*
*efficient utilization of calories and nutrients—*
*if you follow it most of the time.*

In a nation where a television commercial advises you to take an antacid *before* you eat dinner, it's a small wonder that the antidote to being overweight, is often as pernicious as overeating. There are diets that starve you, promise "miracles," guarantee weight reduction in a week, or give you a "full meal in a can." Product marketers are masterful at allurement. We're promised ways to feel better, but deep inside we know there's no shortcut. Over time, the attraction to these new possibilities becomes a habit and our new reality is moving from one possibility to the next.

We know, though, that there are few diet miracles; any "shortcuts" to obtain results are not necessarily the best for us. Getting thinner does not necessarily mean getting healthier. In my program, losing weight is secondary to gaining health. Vitality and rejuvenation are the goals, not shedding pounds.

The *Radiance Diet* teaches us to be flexible with food, based on the theory that what, when, and how much we eat affects our physical, emotional, and psychological well being. For example, you can't be physically and mentally flexible if you're not "food flexible." The recipes in the *Radiance Diet* are nutritionally sound and delicious, but don't hesitate to try out other ingredients on the theory that you can learn to explore your psyche if you learn to experiment with food.

I've included many spices and herbs; if you find new ones, try them, and write to me about their effects. Realize that you're not expected to give up your old food friends. Instead, eat them at noon when your metabolism burns the strongest.

The *Radiance Diet* I have created in this book will allow you to derive maximum benefits from the foods you eat, with the most efficient utilization of calories and nutrients—if you follow it most of the time.

(Sometimes you may "digress" even at night, and occasionally you may overeat. What's important is to follow the diet as a general rule.)

I recognize that everyone is unique; your diet is in many ways very personal to you. You will learn to balance your own diet without needing to copy anyone else's. You'll discover that once you're following the plan, it can be adapted to fit into your lifestyle with maximum benefits for your specific needs. Best of all, your improved energy and vitality are the benefits. Our bodies are uniquely our own; what we put into our physical structures and how we use them, must pertain to our own distinctly personal biological requirements.

Here is an outline of what I consider an ideal diet:

**Upon arising**: Morning Rejuvenator (fresh lemon juice) mixed with warm water

**Breakfast:** Fruit juice, fruit, toasted oats, almond milk, green tea, bancha tea, black tea or kukicha tea (Menopausal women will particularly benefit from almond milk on oats.)

**Lunch:** *Eat the bulk of your food at this time!* If you're just starting the program, go ahead and include your "comfort" foods. Be sure you eat cooked vegetables, especially the green leafy ones. Add whole grains—pasta, rice, or bread. If you are gluten sensitive, make adjustments. For a protein source, focus on those of vegetable origin like beans and non-GMO fermented tofu (though if you crave meat, eat it in moderation, accompanied by vegetables). If you want a beverage with antioxidants, opt for green tea.

**Dinner:** Enjoy mixed vegetables, rice, and a salad. The addition of fish like salmon (four ounces or so) is fine. For a vegetarian option, beans or tempeh are good choices. Stay away from refined carbohydrates.

**Snacks:** Fresh fruits, fresh juices, and herbal teas between meals

**Supplements:** Herbs, flower essences, vitamins and minerals

Before I get into the specifics, I want to talk about one of the most essential elements in my program: not eating anything at all—the overnight fast.

## THE OVERNIGHT FAST

A lot has been written about fasting, much of it is as good for you as junk food. The overall principle is the same, though, in all of the literature—the body needs time to rest and cleanse from the daily activity of digestion.

Fasting has been the subject of much of my research for more than four decades. My understanding and knowledge regarding the physiology of fasting and its psychological effects come from both research studies and from personal experience. Personally I have fasted numerous times and always kept journals of my experience.

(Example: Day 2: *Today I feel like quitting. I am thinking about all the good food I could be eating.* Morning, Day 5: *I feel like a new person. My skin has a glow to it. My eyes are clear. My hunger has not returned yet. It left on Day 3.*)

Here's what I've discovered about fasting:

When we stop eating, our body goes into autolysis (self-digestion) after the first three days. It begins to break down much of its worn-out, aged tissue, and it eliminates toxins through the bowels and skin. Drinking plenty of pure water is vital during a fast, and

I found that fresh, diluted fruit and vegetable juices, which help with cleansing and nourishment, kept me feeling vital.

Most people fast for the wrong reasons and don't recognize the possible side effects. Lengthy fasting is *not* the ideal way to restore health or lose weight (though you *will* lose weight). Sudden fasts are just as bad, as they send the body into shock, almost like showering in ice water after a vigorous exercise.

A critical time comes after the fast ends. The "faster," proud of themselves and having lost a pound or two, may immediately begin to binge on the very foods that they indulged in before the fast. "I can eat again," they tell themselves, "and if I gain too much weight, I can always go on another fast."

Fasting is not a technique to be used to negate bad eating habits. The fast-famine cycle puts a strain on your entire system. I recall Amelia, a client delighted with the new wave of "intermittent fasting." She told me she ate anything she wanted for three days, then fasted for two, then ate a limited diet for one day followed by another day of fasting.

"And I don't have to give up my coffee," she told me proudly.

I noted that Amelia's menstrual cycle, though, was irregular and she suffered from water retention. Her mind was unsteady and anxious at times and she felt vaguely unstable, despite having a good job and pleasant physical surroundings.

Amelia's method of eating and fasting sent her body into a metabolic imbalance. In effect, her liver could not keep up with the changes and the toxins. The body works optimally when it is on a regular schedule, with few, if any surprises. Regularity is the best way to cultivate energy and vitality, since the endocrine organs are the first to shut down when the body is in shock. I introduced Amelia to the overnight fast. She found that by fasting at night she would wake up more refreshed and able to maintain regular meal times. This new schedule helped her to feel balanced and find food more enjoyable. I have successfully used the overnight fast with students and clients since my first book publication, *Sexual Radiance.*[1]

As we've seen, the overnight fast, lasting from 6 p.m. to breakfast (which is not eaten immediately upon rising), gives the body time to cleanse itself. People like to fast—it makes them feel renewed. However, if they do it for long periods, their metabolism will become imbalanced. With the overnight fast, there is no such tendency, and the therapeutic value is greater. The overnight fast leads to a gradual decrease in appetite rather than to the food cravings one feels after an extended fast. It provides enough time for the digestive system to rest in preparation for the morning's rejuvenation; you wake up more refreshed with a sharper mind

Researchers feel that the overnight fast, as described here, may contribute to cell renewal to counter oxidative DNA damage caused by free radicals.[2] You'll be rejuvenating your metabolism. If you do not allow yourself to eat every time your mind tells you that a bite of food would go good just about now, you will be training your mind.

When you wake up your digestion will have been self-cleaning for some twelve hours. Now let's do the math: in the course of twenty-one days, you'd be "fasting" for nearly eleven of them! Break the fast with fresh fruit juice if you feel you need more of a cleansing. In the event that you *did* eat late the night before; you can also opt for the more cleansing fruit juice. The best choice upon waking of course, would be the Morning Rejuvenator.

# QUALITY

You already know that not all food is created equal. Canned beans are inferior to fresh; orange juice from the carton, not as nutritious as fresh-squeezed. The quality of our food has a direct effect on how our body responds and digests it. Even our emotional outlook is affected. I elaborate more on this in my book, *Feeling Good Matters: The Yoga of Mind, Medicine and Healing.*[3] The *Radiance Diet* provides recipes based on whole foods (fresh, non-GMO and chemical-free) as much as possible, but this does not mean you have to be an organic farmer or move your residence from city to countryside.

Good food is not only found in special health food markets (though it is fun to forage in them periodically). There are many quality fresh fruits and vegetables offered in supermarkets and local farm stands today that will enable you to eat healthfully. Indeed, you can eat well even if you're backpacking. I take along pre-packaged dried beans, add water to them, cook for six minutes, and have a nutritious dish, even if it's not gourmet cuisine.

You needn't eat only raw vegetables. Steaming your vegetables with the correct spices will break down the fibers, make the food more digestible, and its vitamins more bioavailable. You must start out with fresh foods and then work from there.

**A few hints will help you move toward energy and vitality:**

*Grains* should be roasted to make them more digestible. Try barley, brown rice, oats, millet, quinoa, rye, buckwheat, wild rice, and whole wheat. (Obtain gluten-free grains if needed.)

*Fats* are required for metabolic function to repair cell membranes. Fish oils, cold-pressed sesame oil, coconut oil, olive oil, and ghee—clarified butter—are all metabolic enhancers. Some other high quality fats are found in lower-mercury fish and seafood, such as salmon, shrimp, cod, and sardines, in addition to wild game, avocados, almonds, pecans, pine nuts, walnuts, pumpkin and sunflower seeds.

Avoid higher-mercury fish, such as tilefish from the Gulf of Mexico, shark, swordfish, and king mackerel. *Essential proteins* can come from meats, fish, or vegetable combinations; the *Radiance Diet* includes them all. In general, avoid beef and be aware that all meats are highly acidifying; many are contaminated with steroids and antibiotics. Stick to wild game, free-range poultry, and seafood; and while you are at it, use animal protein in moderation. From the legume menu, choose lentils, mung beans, black beans, white beans, navy beans, kidney beans, pinto beans, lima beans, chickpeas, split peas, and as an alternative to tofu, choose tempeh and miso.

*Dairy products* on the whole should be limited, especially soft cheeses. It is not necessarily the best source of calcium for most people—kale, ground sesame seeds, kelp, sardines, broccoli, and almonds can supply it better. If you need to drink milk choose organic, and you may want to consider raw milk; although it is suggested to boil it first. Fresh yogurt is good because it contains lactobacillus acidophilus, a probiotic that feeds your gut flora.

*Vegetables, roots, fruits, and seaweeds* perform miracles in the body, but they're insufficient without proteins and fats.

*Table salt* should be avoided, so use *celtic* salt or wheat-free tamari instead.

*Processed foods* should be eliminated.

*Refined sugar* should be taken in minimum amounts, if at all, there are plenty of substitutes: applesauce, fruits, molasses, coconut sugar, honey (honey is not only sweet, but it's packed with an array of health benefits), and maple syrup (maple syrup contains a fair bit of sugar, so consume it rather minimally).

# QUANTITY

While it's better to eat lots of healthy foods than it is to consume a moderate amount of unhealthy ones, it's still true that the less you eat (within reason), the more weight you'll lose (if that is your goal) and the more vital you'll feel.

To cut down on the quantity of food you eat:

- Chew until solid food becomes liquid—well, *almost* liquid. There's no need to be fanatical.
- Start the meal by eating whole foods. You'll automatically cut down on how much you can consume. Whole foods are far more filling.
- Don't eat one food item completely and separately, followed by another food. Start by sample tasting each one,

and then rotate them. When we eat one food alone and exclusively, we are rarely satisfied.

- Eat your favorite foods first (most kids and many adults save them for last).
- Balance each meal by combining acid foods with alkaline ones. Start with the alkalizing, such as greens and then continue with other choices on your plate. The urge to binge will disappear.
- Include herbs and spices. Many times we eat too much due to a desire for some flavor. For example, if you just eat plain rice, you'll want more flavorful food. Spice the rice up with curry or peanut sauce, and you'll be more satisfied.
- Avoid cold foods and drinks. These lead to overeating. If you drink ice water, you'll want to overeat, so switch to water at room temperature or opt for warm tea. Kukicha (twig) tea will cut sugar cravings. You can find it at any health-food store.
- When you feel as if you *must* have a bowl of ice cream at night, promise yourself you can have it the next day, at noon, when your digestive fire is highest.

Of course, there will always be times when you're unable to resist your urges. For those times when you do overeat try the following remedies:

- Don't be too hard on yourself, you *are* human.
- Drink warm ginger, fennel tea, or kukicha tea, which will counteract the acidity of too much dessert.
- Drink peppermint tea to help digest fats.

- Chew on fennel seeds. (Don't swallow them.)
- Fast when it's normally time for your evening meal; opt for fresh vegetable juice or broth.
- To reprogram your taste buds, drink dandelion root tea. Its bitters operate on the small intestine, an organ most affected by overeating. If the tea is too strong, try a dried-extract capsule.
- Go back to the *Radiance Diet* for an extended period.

## SUPPLEMENTS

If you follow the *Radiance Diet*, you still might need supplements due to external factors. Some reasons include: many foods are grown in soil depleted of nutrients such as zinc or selenium; perhaps you are eating too many processed foods; or maybe you've been overusing the microwave.

Remember, though, that a supplement does not contain or replace the live, organic nutrients found in "real" whole food. Don't overestimate the power of vitamins.

When deciding on a supplement, opt for a high-potency multiple. You want the synergistic action of the multi-vitamin. I don't recommend isolating vitamins by taking them separately, since there's a possibility you'll create imbalance; this can do you more harm than good.

You'll want to make sure your multiple contains the correct amounts, so you'll have to learn to read a label. It's a good idea to get a well-respected vitamin book as an adjunct to this one.

Remember:

- Each of us is biologically and physiologically unique based upon our genes, our experiences, and our lifestyles. A supplement that is good for one person, may not be as good for another.
- Manufacturers are prone to make extravagant claims (and use sophisticated marketing techniques) for the thousands of supplements they produce. Don't take them at face value.
- *With the help of a professional,* determine your needs, establish your objectives, and use the supplements systematically, not just when you feel like it.
- If you do decide on a multiple vitamin, eliminate it for one day each week to clean out any buildup of the fat-soluble vitamins.
- Vitamins and other micronutrients support out biochemical processes and don't create immediate, or drastic changes, in the body. Give yourself three to four weeks to notice any changes. If none seem to occur, re-consult with your medical provider.
- *Never self-diagnose!*

Vitamins and minerals that specifically enhance vitality are:
*Vitamin A* - required for healthy epithelial and mucosal cells; it has also been shown to increase progesterone levels. A deficiency of vitamin A is associated with decreased thyroid levels.

Beta-carotene- converted to vitamin A, it is an essential nutrient. It has antioxidant activity, which helps to protect cells from damage.

*B vitamins* - support the nervous system and mental performance, contribute to normal energy metabolism, aid psychological and neurological function and help reduce tiredness and fatigue.

*Bioflavonoids* - antioxidants that have a strong estrogenic effect and support the cell membranes.

*Vitamin C* - an antioxidant that strengthens cell walls and is required for progesterone secretion.

*Vitamin E* - an important vitamin required for the proper function of many organs in the body. It is also an antioxidant. This means it helps to slow down processes that damage cells.

*Calcium* - good for the nervous system and healthy bone function.

*Magnesium* - activates enzymes to metabolize amino acids and promotes utilization of other vitamins in maintaining the acid/base balance.

*Selenium* - helps protect the body from environmental toxins and is good for the thyroid, which affects libido.

*Zinc* - vital for the proper functioning of the immune system.

**Note:** Reminder, don't mix and match vitamins and minerals on your own!

## HERBS

Herbs perform many different biochemical functions in the body. Some enhance digestion, others eliminate fatigue. Some help clean the liver, others restore adrenals. Some stimulate blood flow, others shield against toxins. Many maintain or increase energy and vitality. In some of the recipes of the *Radiance Diet*, you'll often find herbs included as part of the ingredients.

Herbs can be taken supplementally as well. My only caution is to read the labels if the herb comes pre-packaged, and I suggest that you buy your herbs from reputable companies. Herbs are potent. Some are even toxic (however, those are not listed in this book). I would caution against mixing too many therapeutic doses of herbs at one time, for they might not complement one another.

If you're just becoming familiar with herbs, it is best to observe and judge your body's response by starting with herb teas, which are less potent than whole dried extracts. If herbs seem to suit you, go on to fresh herbs or dried herbs, but make sure you don't use anything beyond its expiration date. Spices should not be more than six months old. Herbs may have a longer shelf life depending on how they were processed. By the expiration date, though, the herb may have lost its therapeutic value.

---

*Here are ten spices and herbs used specifically to ignite metabolism and aid the digestive system:*

| | |
|---|---|
| Black peppercorn | Fennel |
| Cardamom | Garlic |
| Cayenne pepper | Ginger |
| Cinnamon | Long Pepper (Pippali) |
| Coriander | Turmeric |
| Cumin | |

---

Spices and herbs like these can be mixed to your liking, but try not to overdo the hot, stimulating ones often used to help digestion. Both black peppercorn and cardamom, for example, aid digestion, but one stimulates while the other calms it.

## Herbs Specifically Beneficial to
## Vital Health are the Following:

**Ashwagandha** (*Withania somnifera*) is often recommended for various kinds of disease processes, thyroid support and especially helpful as a nervine tonic.

**Brahmi** (*Bacopa monnieri*) is commonly used for Alzheimer's disease, to improve memory, relieve anxiety, and for attention deficit-hyperactivity disorder (ADHD), among its many other uses.

*Note: not to be confused with gotu kola and other natural medicines that are also sometimes called brahmi—which might increase certain brain chemicals.*

**Dandelion** (*Taraxacum officinale*) moves the blood, regulates hormones, and acts beneficially on liver function.

**Dong quai** (*Angelica sinensis*) often called the "female ginseng," is considered a rejuvenating female tonic and hormone regulator.

**Ginger** (*Zingiber officinale*) balances the eicosanoids, those substances responsible for keeping metabolism in balance.

**Gotu kola** (*Centella asiatica*) is considered one of the most important rejuvenative herbs in Ayurvedic medicine; it strengthens the adrenals and purifies the blood.

**Licorice** (*Glycyrrhiza glabra*) acts as a rejuvenator of the endocrine system.

**Milk thistle** (*Silybum marianum*) strengthens the liver and protects against environmental toxins.

**Siberian ginseng** (*Eleutherococcus senticosus*) supports the adrenals and nervous system.

**St. John's wort** (*Hypericum perforatum*) a mood elevator can help relieve depression and anxiety.

**Turmeric** (*Curcuma longa*) regulates hormone function and promotes proper metabolism.

**Wild yam** (*Dioscorea villosa*) is an essential source of zinc.

## FLOWER ESSENCES

Unlike herbs, flower essences work on an energetic level and can rejuvenate and revitalize. They can be added to "the diet," not as additional food but especially as aids to psychological well-being. I've seen remarkable results with a single essence as well as combinations. Be mindful that if you are using these essences for the first time it is best to limit combinations. However, I suggest that if you're interested in pursuing flower essences further, consult a professional practitioner. There are many types of flower essences from around the world. A comprehensive book on the how to use various flower essences for spiritual and emotional well-being is *Healing with Flower Essences*, by Joan Greenblatt. A good book on the subject of North American essences is *Flower Essence Repertory: A Comprehensive Guide to North American and English*

*Flower Essences for Emotional and Spiritual Well-Being,* by Patricia Kaminski and Richard Katz.[4] Among the flower essences I recommend are: **pink yarrow,** particularly effective during menopause; **arnica** for the recovery of energy after trauma; **evening primrose,** to assist with creating intimacy; **hibiscus** to aid warmth and responsiveness in female sexuality; **lady's slipper,** to help balance the lower chakras; and **snapdragon,** for the development of a strong libido.

One recipe, using North American essences that I've found particularly helpful for awakening vitality is this:

In 1 oz. of distilled water, add:

2 drops of brandy (a preservative)

2 drops of self-heal flower essence

2 drops of hibiscus flower essence

2 drops of crab apple flower essence

Mix, and take 2 to 4 drops under the tongue four times a day. Do not mix with food fifteen minutes before or after consumption. If you're experiencing distress in your life, replace the hibiscus with arnica.

## ESSENTIAL OILS

Essential oils are created from compounds extracted from plants; they are made from the essence of their basic source, and are most commonly used as a tool in aromatherapy. Due to their highly concentrated nature, essential oils are **not meant to be ingested.**[5] It is advised to avoid using these oils internally, especially if prescribed by a lay practitioner, whose education may be primarily from a marketing focus, and not from a clinical perspective. It is far safer to follow the advice regarding ingestion from a licensed physician properly trained in specific dosing of essential oils.[6] There is a high probability of developing extreme gastric distress or hyperacidity if you ingest these oils. When used in an external application, do not apply full-strength essential oils directly to the skin. Due to the highly-concentrated nature of essential oils and their chemical components, it is advised to never apply these products directly to the skin without first being diluted with a carrier oil. The other best utilization of these oils is in a diffuser. Caution, though, must be used with essential oils and these populations: pregnant women, infants and children, especially those with respiratory issues. Diffuser use with infants or young children may be unsafe dependent upon the type of essential oil being utilized.[7] Do your research.

I include essential oils here because they have the propensity to elevate mood. I use oils all the time in my bath, or when getting or receiving a massage. They smell wonderful, relieve stress, relax the body, and quiet the mind, and if you've eaten well, they'll even enhance your mood. For example:

**Basil,** in an aromatic nerve tonic, is used to reduce mental fatigue due to stress.

**Chamomile** relaxes the body by calming the nerves.

**Frankincense** has an uplifting effect on the body and mind; it is used to clarify spaces to promote healthy moods.

**Jasmine** elevates mood and induces euphoria. It's commonly used as an aphrodisiac.

**Lavender** reduces stress and relieves headaches.

**Neroli**, among the finest flower essences, makes a luxurious and relaxing bath or massage oil.

**Rose** stimulates a feeling of well-being.

**Rosemary** clears the mind.

**Sandalwood** relaxes and calms the mind and body.

**Ylang-ylang**, called the "flower of flowers," is commonly used as an aphrodisiac and is one of the most emotionally-evocative essential oils.

Be aware of the potential side effects from essential oil use, and discontinue if you experience any of these: nausea, asthmatic attacks, allergic reactions, rashes, or severe headaches. Experiment with them, though. What will smell good to one person may not be so appealing to another. Different aromas will have unique psychological and chemical reactions for each person, based upon their individual constitution. The experimentation is an interesting adventure, one that often proves widely insightful.

## THE RADIANCE DIET

Diet, breathing, exercise and meditation are so important. This is why the *Return to Radiance* program will rekindle your vital life. I have said it before, a lack of radiance is often the result of an unhealthy body and imbalanced mind.

*Here's how* The Radiance Diet *plan relates specifically to vitality:*

1. A vital body requires protein and minerals. The *Radiance*

*Diet* includes protein from a number of lean sources, and an abundance of minerals from fresh fruits and vegetables.

2. Engaging in life requires stamina. The *Radiance Diet* provides the whole grains to balance blood-glucose levels, thus enhancing endurance.

3. Vitality is controlled by hormones secreted by the endocrine glands. The *Radiance Diet* guarantees them proper nutrition.

4. The pituitary gland has both direct and indirect effects on sexual and reproductive functions. Any pituitary deficiency causes underdeveloped sex organs, impotence (in men), and early menopause. The *Radiance Diet* recommends foods and vitamin supplements (the B-complex vitamins, vitamin E, zinc, niacin, and so on) specifically for the care and feeding of this essential gland.

5. We've seen that the adrenal glands are the seat of vitality. These glands also need vitamin-rich foods and supplements. Moreover, I've made sure that this diet avoids certain foods, such as refined sugar and white flour products.

6. The thyroid gland is correlated with metabolic strength. Iodine and several vitamins are essential for the production of its hormones. That's why the *Radiance Diet* includes seafood and vegetables.

7. The B vitamins—thiamine, riboflavin, niacin, folic acid, vitamin B12, biotin—vitamin E, and zinc are essential for the brain's production of neurotransmitters. This diet will supply them.

8. Vital energy can be adversely affected by many things, in-

cluding drugs, alcohol, caffeine, and many common medicines. The *Radiance Diet* will rejuvenate your system—but only if you quit using the substances that sapped your vitality in the first place.

———————○———————

If you follow the *Radiance Diet*, you will feel better, look healthier, *be* healthier, and have more energy in your daily life. You'll see its greatest effects, though, by your ability to remain calm and clear in stressful situations. Your mood will be dramatically enhanced if you learn to breathe properly, exercise—particularly your solar plexus—and if you meditate.

# CHAPTER 10

───────○───────

# Breathing for Vitality

*Yoga masters recognized thousands of years ago that
by regulating their breath, they would gain access
to controlling their health and longevity.*

Michele came into my meditation seminar to overcome her anxiety and learn to relax. Right away I noticed that she was breathing from her chest, and her nose was not clear enough to breathe well. She appeared to be gasping for air, so it's little wonder she was uncomfortable and anxious.

As I began the seminar, I asked Michele to lie on her mat, facedown, so that she would be activating her diaphragm to breathe. She did so, and within a few minutes expressed how relaxed she already felt. Then I asked her to turn over and practice the same diaphragmatic breathing while on her back. She quickly understood the practice and continued to relax and feel better.

For the next part of the exercise, "come to a comfortable, upright seated position and establish diphragmatic breathing."

I explained that balancing the breath balances the brain, and that the way Michele had been breathing before—using her chest—agitated her nervous system and had elicited a sympathetic "anxious" response.

If you master your breath, you *master* your health. It's as simple as that. This powerful statement is true for several reasons:

- Breath is the vehicle for prana, or vital energy, that is supplied to the brain.

- When we have conscious control over our breath, we are able to regulate all the vital energy centers within the brain as well as the body.

- The way we breathe determines the health of all our organs, especially the brain, because of the breath's ability to regulate the autonomic nervous system via the sympathetic and parasympathetic branches.

- The way we breathe determines the brain's health. If you breathe smoothly, it will influence the mind field by producing harmony; in contrast, pauses or jerkiness in breathing patterns produce irritation and instability in the mind. For example: you may remember a time while swimming when you were forced to hold your breath too long and your mind panicked. That's because the pause between your exhalation and inhalation elicited an alarm signal to the nervous system alerting that you might be in danger. This is a longer pause than you normally experience everyday. However, this kind of pause may indeed happen at any time and causes unsteadiness in the mind field. A systematic meditation practice that focuses on steadying the breath is the antidote to the "pause" problem. Paying attention to exhalation and inhalation as a continuous cycle will ameliorate the consequences of unsteady breath, thereby helping to balance the mind as well as the nervous system.

- Breath links us to Spirit. The word "spirit" comes from the Latin root *spirare*, which means "to breathe." Life is breathed into us at birth; and at death, when we expire, the breath leaves, along with the Spirit.

Breathing connects all systems in our bodies by way of the parasympathetic and sympathetic branches of our nervous system. Nothing happens in our bodies without breath. The heart can't pump, the brain can't function, hormones can't flow, and so on. Breathe incorrectly and you will be harming all systems of the body. Breathe correctly and you will be far along on the road to vitality.

Look at any child from ages one to five, and you'll see that he or she breathes from the diaphragm—the muscle that separates the upper body from the lower. It's the natural way to breathe, yet as we grow older and are subjected to anxiety, stress, and fear, our breathing shifts to the chest, and thereby creates unnecessary arousal and sympathetic activity. Physiologists call this a sympathetic (fight-or-flight) response.

The purpose of this chapter is to teach you a more natural way to breathe, a way that maximizes respiratory efficiency, and creates balance in the autonomic nervous system. It's the very way you should breathe when you relax, or listen to soothing music. It's the way you should breathe if you want to bring the mind back to its home-base, and experience peace and tranquility—it is called diaphragmatic breathing.

I started teaching diaphragmatic breathing many decades ago. At that time I was working solely with women to help them regulate their metabolism through diet, movement, and meditation. With the purpose of activating metabolism and mental rejuvenation, I taught clients and students to begin with diaphragmatic breathing—a smooth, unbroken expansion of the lungs that begins at the bottom of the lungs, not at the top. With practice, this method of breathing will become the way you always breathe, as you did when you were born. Diaphragmatic breathing cuts down on the number of breaths per minute, saves work on the heart, and boosts blood circulation by sending blood coursing strongly throughout the system. When the diaphragm is fully expanded, the intercostal muscles open the rib cage and fill the mid-lungs with air, resulting in optimal oxygen exchange. The exercises that follow are taken from both ancient and modern sources. They have been modified in some cases to make them easier for the average person (you and me), but they'll revitalize you.

## DIAPHRAGMATIC BREATHING

The human body was designed for diaphragmatic breathing, but many of us have diaphragms that do not move, they are frozen.

This limits sensitivity and awareness, and increases stress. If you are a chest breather, I guarantee that you feel anxious and agitated, as opposed to calm and energized.

Diaphragmatic breathing is both energizing and relaxing. The breathing apparatus includes the trachea, which allows air to pass into the lungs; the lungs are the organs where gas exchange takes place; the diaphragm, which lengthens and shortens the chest cavity; and the rib cage, which creates the structure and protection of the breathing apparatus.

The diaphragm is a resilient, flexible, muscular membrane that separates the chest cavity from the abdominal cavity. When the lungs expand, they push the diaphragm downward; when the lungs contract, they pull it toward the chest cavity. During diaphragmatic breathing, the chest has little to no movement, and the abdomen moves slightly. As you refine and perfect your breathing, this motion becomes increasingly subtle.

## DIAPHRAGMATIC BREATHING EXERCISE

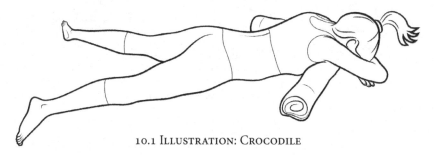

10.1 ILLUSTRATION: CROCODILE

*Purpose*

*To establish diaphragmatic breathing. This exercise is the foundation for all exercises that follow.*

## DIAPHRAGMATIC BREATHING TECHNIQUE

1. We begin in the Crocodile Pose (*Makarasana*). In this pose, you rest on the abdomen with a rolled-up blanket across the upper chest and under the armpits. This supports the upper body so you can relax the neck, shoulders, and upper back into the position. The head rests on the folded arms, above and under the front of the head. The legs are about 6-10 inches apart, with the feet turned out or in, based on the preference for comfort.

2. Rest here and begin inhaling and exhaling. As you inhale, you'll feel the abdomen press into the floor and the back expand and rise. As you exhale, the abdomen will contract and relax and the back will sink and relax. You may also notice that the rib cage will expand on the inhale and contract and relax on the exhale.

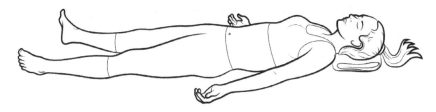

10.2 ILLUSTRATION: SUPINE

3. Now, roll over onto the back. In this pose, called the "Corpse Pose" (*Shavasana*), rest on the back with a thin cushion under the head to keep the neck neutral, with the head in alignment with the spine. If you have back dis-

comfort, you can place a rolled blanket or a bolster under the knees to take the stress off the psoas muscle and relax the back. The arms are placed slightly away from the body, and the fingers are facing upward. Legs are in a relaxed, comfortable position 6-10 inches apart—again, based on your comfort.

4. Rest here, inhaling and exhaling. As you inhale, you'll feel the abdomen expand as if you're filling a balloon. As you exhale, your abdomen will relax and deflate. You may feel the ribs expand (ever so slightly toward the back) on an inhale, and contract on an exhale.

5. If you have difficulty feeling the abdomen move, you may extend your arms and hands over your head. This immobilizes the chest making you unable to use those muscles while inhaling and exhaling.

---○---

Do this practice for 5-10 minutes daily until you feel comfortable and relaxed in this breathing position. (As you become more advanced and want to strengthen the diaphragm muscle, you can use a sandbag. I recommend you work with a teacher to show you its exact positioning.)

Next, we move onto alternate nostril breathing. We begin with the nostrils. As noted, most people are oblivious to which nostril is dominant at any given time. If you came to me feeling lethargic and uninterested in life, my first question would be, "Which nostril feels more air flow?" If you didn't know, my next statement would be, "Once you become aware of the dominant nostril flow, then you will be better able to change your present physical state." Nostril breathing should be deep, slow, constant, smooth, natural, regular, silent, and gentle—with an inhalation/exhalation ratio of 1:1.

I've already discussed the benefits of alternate-nostril breathing; now you will learn why it is important, and how to practice. Nasal breathing is much preferred to mouth breathing for a variety of reasons. The inner part of the nose performs nearly thirty functions, among them the filtering, warming, and moisturizing of incoming air. It is responsible for the ability to smell, which affects the limbic system—the seat of emotion.

## ALTERNATE-NOSTRIL BREATHING EXERCISE

*Purpose*
*To alternate the flow of air between the right and left nostrils, thereby balancing the energy channels associated with the right and left nostril, as well as the right and left hemispheres of the brain. Once mastered, it is an excellent means for focusing and calming the mind.*

10.3 ILLUSTRATION: BREATHING

## ALTERNATE-NOSTRIL BREATHING TECHNIQUE

1. Sit in a chair, with head, neck, and trunk aligned.
2. Bring your right hand to the nose, folding the pinky, index finger, and middle finger so that the right thumb can be used to close the right nostril and the ring finger can be used to close the left nostril.
3. Close the left nostril and exhale completely through the right nostril.
4. At the end of the exhalation, close the right nostril and slowly inhale through the left nostril. Inhalation and exhalation should be of equal duration.
5. Repeat the cycle of exhalation with the right nostril and inhalation with the left nostril three times.
6. At the end of the third inhalation with the left nostril, exhale completely through the *same* nostril, while keeping the right nostril closed with the finger or thumb.
7. At the end of exhalation, close the left nostril and inhale through the right nostril.
8. Exhale through the left nostril and inhale through the right three times.
9. Place your hands on your knees and exhale and inhale through both nostrils evenly, for three complete breaths.

This completes one cycle of alternate-nostril breathing. You should be fully aware of the process. At the beginning, repeat 3 rounds in the morning and 3 rounds at night.

## 2:1 BREATHING EXERCISE

*Purpose*
*To expel toxins from the body and rejuvenate the energy system.*

Yoga masters recognized thousands of years ago that by regulating their breath, they would gain access to controlling their health and longevity. Currently, informed health care practitioners, knowing its health benefits, recommend diaphragmatic breathing to their patients and clients.

Diaphragmatic breathing coordinated with an even steady flow of breath at a ratio of 2 exhalations to 1 inhalation (or 2:1) is designed to expel stale residual air and toxins from the deepest recesses of the lungs, in order to clear and open all passages in the throat and head (this is especially valuable for smokers and city dwellers). The associated rise in oxygen levels revitalizes the blood, and as oxygen travels throughout the body it stimulates the metabolism. Extra oxygen calms the nervous system, stimulates digestion, and is beneficial to the adrenal glands. Diaphragmatic breathing is something you should do consistently all day, and is an important aid in activating the solar plexus; it will actually help the digestion process after a very large meal. **2:1 breathing** is a practice that you can incorporate into your lifestyle routine to enhance your vitality and rejuvenate.

---

## 2.1 BREATHING TECHNIQUE

1. Sit with the head, neck, and trunk in a straight line.
2. Place your tongue against the roof of your mouth and keep it there throughout the exercise.
3. Begin by exhaling through the nostrils, to a count of four.
4. Immediately afterward, gently inhale through the nostrils to a count of two.
5. Repeat this exercise for one to three minutes. End with complete inhalation and exhalation. You can change the count of your exhalation and inhalation according to your capacity.
6. Do not practice this breath while exercising.

---

# CHAPTER 11

———————○———————

# Exercises That Energize

*Awareness is the first step in changing any*
*aspect of yourself, and exercise is a great*
*way to become aware of your body.*

Courtney came to see me for an appointment. She felt like she was carrying excess weight around her abdomen, hips, and thighs, and she wanted to put together a workout to meet her particular needs. Her diet was reasonable, I found, though we made a few adjustments. When I asked her about her moods and emotions, she claimed that she felt older than her years. She was slouching and breathing from her chest, an obvious reflection of the condition of her mind.

I invited Courtney to come to the mat.

"Please lie down on the mat, face down," I said.

"Let's begin by establishing diaphragmatic breathing."

After I demonstrated, Courtney seemed eager to try.

"With your body face down, be aware of your lower back, rising and falling as you inhale and exhale."

She began the practice, as was evident by the rising and falling action of her back.

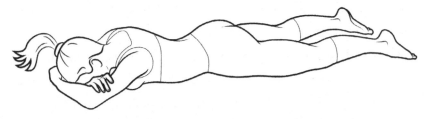

11.1 Illustration: Crocodile Pose (*Markrasana*)

Next I said to Courtney, " Roll onto your back with your feet on the floor, and watch the rise and fall of your abdomen as you inhale and exhale."

This was a bit more difficult for her.

After a few weeks, Courtney learned how to use her diaphragm muscle to breathe. It wasn't long before she reported that she did not feel the emotional fluctuations that seemed to be at the root of her anxiety. Eventually, she was able to stabilize her moods and started to feel good about herself.

The first part of starting any of my programs, as outlined in this book, is to establish diaphragmatic breathing, so that movement will have the added benefit of rejuvenating the entire body, mind, and spirit. If you follow the exercises prescribed here along with a good diet and breathing (as I continue to remind you—for the three are inextricably intertwined), you will feel your body move effortlessly with lightness and energy. These are exercises that reduce stress and tension, because the aim here is to activate your hub of resilience—the abdominal-pelvic center. When we shut down our solar plexus, we diminish our life force. When we activate this center, we find our entire selves vitalized.

Mind you, I have nothing against cardiovascular activities if done skillfully with awareness, but most of us do them without the awareness of our breath flow. If you find yourself bent-over huffing and puffing on a StairMaster or Treadmill, make sure that you are not putting unnecessary stress on the body as opposed to building it up. I recommend t'ai chi and yoga for their physical effects, but mostly because they help maintain a balance between mind and body. Be sure your instructor, in either of these disciplines, is aware of the importance of the breath. I also endorse lifting weights because it is important to have strong bones and upper-body strength, to maintain a solid foundation, and to walk in alignment. All of these have their place. The exercises that I suggest here build a foundation for vital energy.

Awareness is the first step in changing any aspect of yourself, and exercise is a great way to become aware of your body. However, it is essential to remember that exercise or movement and breathing are inextricably intertwined; be sure to read the chapter on breath before starting the exercises I recommend.

The *Return to Radiance* program begins with your posture. Many of us have a locked sacral region due to excessive sitting and tension. You must learn to stand straight and walk in a manner that allows your hips to flow with the rest of your body. Unless you can do this, your vitality will be limited and the exercises won't have their full effect.

The exercises here are designed to help realign your body. When your spinal column is not straight and steady, both psychological and physiological issues can arise. When we're depressed, for example, we tend to let our head droop. This posture will in turn create a feedback loop that will keep us in a depressed state. Unless you extend the spine and hold your head, neck, and trunk straight, your breathing will be affected, as well as your mood. A balanced body provides the foundation for balance on every level of our being, including the energy, mind, and spirit.

Before starting the exercises, try "body scanning." Later in the chapter, I'll teach you the optimum method, but for now, take a moment and try this simple scanning technique. See if you are able to detect different sensations throughout your body. Does the left side of your face feel the same as the right side? Do your shoulders feel heavy or light? When you stand, do both feet put equal pressure on the floor, or are you favoring one more than the other? As you become more aware of how your body feels, it will be easier to balance yourself through exercise.

Finally, there are the exercises themselves. These exercises are designed to develop muscles without stiffness, so that energy runs freely to revitalize the organs, such as the liver, kidneys, and the lungs, as well as the reproductive organs. One aim is to increase respiration in the same way aerobic exercise does. Yoga techniques are employed to incorporate both tension and relaxation in order to keep the subtle energy pathways flowing freely.

## YOUR EXERCISE SELF-EVALUATION

Before beginning any exercise program, you must ask yourself two questions: "What is my goal?" and "How is my health?" The exercises here assume your health is good, and that you want to activate your metabolism so that you can maintain or promote vitality and add longevity to it.

As you exercise, evaluate your appetite for food, and for new adventures, and then keep track of any changes that you experience. Do you become more ravenous for food within two hours of exercising? If so, you're probably exercising too much. Be careful of "rationalizing ideas" that come into your mind sometimes, when working hard in an exercise program. All it takes is the thought, *I've burned off five hundred calories. I deserve a snack,* and you've undone your resolve. These thoughts can actually lead to gaining weight in response to exercising. Does your stress level increase after a week of hard workouts? Again, you're probably exercising too much. In fact, exercise can cause an imbalance if you do it for the wrong reasons. Too much exercise will deplete your essential fluids. Overexercising, particularly in concert with overeating, will cause you to lose the softness and grace that comes with being radiant. Hardness sets in. Passion is driven out. If you find yourself preferring to exercise rather than nourishing yourself, that's a sign you're creating imbalance.

Evaluate your desire for further exercise. If you feel enthusiastic about the next workout, good! If, on the other hand, you drag yourself to the exercise room feeling fatigued and disheartened, take a day off. Or, take two (but don't take three). If you haven't been exercising regularly, you may feel uncomfortable at first, but even if there's a little muscle soreness you can still feel good. Determine for yourself the difference between mildly uncomfortable and needing a rest or recovery period.

## EXERCISE REGULARLY AND SYSTEMATICALLY

Some people are more energetic in the morning, others at night. If possible, exercise when you feel most energetic (before or after work, before breakfast, or after dinner), but be consistent. Discipline means shaping desired behavior. Find what works best for you, not what works for your friends. It's fun to exercise in tandem with a friend, but choose one with a similar energy pattern. You'll both benefit.

In general, exercising in the morning is usually better for those people just starting out, or those who have trouble sticking to a program. As noted, it saves you from having the time to think about not doing it and it fends off excuses like, "I've had a tough day at the office," or "I walked a lot today anyway." As we've seen, one drawback to morning exercise is that you're likely to feel slightly more hungry during the day. Resist the impulse to add more food to your lunch, and avoid the mid-morning snack.

Afternoons are probably the hardest time to exercise, since this is when your blood sugar is low and you may want a quick pick-me-up rather than an hour of working out. However, moderate exercise may deter the binge eating that often occurs in the late afternoon.

Exercising in the evening will relax you, if you do it one to two hours following a light dinner, and don't consume more food afterward. Evening exercise will most likely give you a greater metabolic boost resulting in an increase in weight loss, if this is your goal. The only downside is that you may have trouble sleeping if you become too stimulated during your routine. So it is best to evaluate exercise time and quality of your sleep, then make adjustments.

## DURATION AND FREQUENCY

Pick the best time of your day for exercise, and stick to it for 21 days. That's how long the body takes to adapt to exercise, and to change. After the three weeks are over, evaluate your progress. If you're seeing results, continue at the same pace for the next 14 days, at which time you might want to move on to a more advanced level of exercise.

The American College of Sports Medicine recommends 150 minutes/week to maintain health or improve health.[1] If you translate this to your metabolism, you'll find that the same schedule holds true. There is no permanent change without regular exercise, but remember that moderate, sustained exercise is far better for your health than vigorous exerted exercise.

## SUPPLEMENTARY EXERCISE

The use of weights and other devices—such as extra resistance of any kind during a workout—will increase muscle endurance and strength. They may also increase your heart rate depending on the speed, intensity, and duration of the activity you are using to create resistance. There's no question that this can help develop the muscle, tendon, and ligament strength needed to balance your body. I don't emphasize resistance training in this program—truly you should build up to it over time—but I recognize its importance, and if you think you're up to it, go for it.

As for cardiovascular benefits, this program does include a workout that if performed at the highest level will provide some conditioning. If you want cardiovascular benefits, it is best to add activities such as cycling, fast walking, jogging, or swimming to your weekly routine.

The program includes flexibility training that goes beyond the simple stretching that all of us should do before any extended exercise. Combined with diaphragmatic breathing, it will allow you to direct the physical and mental aspects of your health.

### Exercise Guidelines:
- As you exercise, continue with diaphragmatic breathing.
- Choose the best time of day to do the exercises consistently and systematically. Be flexible with the time you do your exercise at the beginning to see what suits you best.
- Do your exercise on an empty stomach. If that's too difficult, drink a cup of tea or diluted fruit juice before you

start (or perhaps have some yogurt). Remember, it's hard to breathe properly if your digestive system is still working on the last meal.

- Find a clean, well-ventilated room where you can be comfortable. Make sure there are no distractions. Turn off the cell-phone and request some time free from interruptions. As I've said, it's okay to exercise with a friend, but they must be as dedicated as you. If you want music, fine, but make sure it doesn't distract you from your breath awareness.

- Create a habit that will help you continue beyond the first days or weeks. If you feel exhilarated by the exercises, you know you're doing something right. Begin by thinking of these exercises as a way of observing yourself. One of the goals is to change the imbalances in your body (discovered through the body scanning technique), but this takes time.

- Do not be discouraged by the lack of a sudden "emotional lift" or epiphany. The benefits of exercise come in time, and the time will go by faster if you are having fun.

- The exercises outlined here are intended for use by women in good health. If you have a condition that warrants medical attention, get your doctor's okay before starting the program. Pregnant and postpartum women should also check with their doctor first. Some of the breathing techniques are not to be used if you're pregnant or menstruating; therefore, check with your healthcare practitioner before you begin.

# BODY SCANNING

## *Purpose*

*To be aware of where tension resides in your body so you can release it. Once you know where the problems lie, you'll be able to form your own routine of exercises.*

---

## BODY SCANNING TECHNIQUE

1.  Stand or lie down. Allow your feet to be aligned with your hips (your feet will be approximately 12" apart), with your weight evenly balanced over your hips. If you are lying down, your weight will be distributed evenly throughout the body.

2.  Close your eyes and begin scanning by "observing" the lightness or heaviness you feel in various parts of your body.

3.  Start with the head, followed by the neck and upper back.

4.  Continue to the shoulders, arms, hands, hips, pelvis, thighs, knees, calves, and feet.

5.  Remain in your chosen position for three minutes after you've completed the scan; pay close attention to your thought processes. When a thought comes into your awareness, notice the effect it has on your body.

---

# STANDING EXERCISES

*Purpose*

*To build body heat, strength, and endurance. These exercises are designed to increase the flexibility of the legs and upper body while toning the front and back of the thighs, and increase upper-body definition. Bending adds to the flexibility of the spine and promotes vitality.*

**Note:** When women carry weight on their hips and thighs, sometimes they feel less vital. The standing exercises will address this issue by increasing lean muscle tissue and promoting weight loss.

---

## OVERALL STANDING TECHNIQUE

Keep the spine as erect as possible. Maintain a straight posture and avoid slumping. Weight should be evenly distributed through your feet.

---

# CELESTIAL BREATH

*Purpose*
*Balancing the mind-body connection.*

———————————○———————————

## CELESTIAL BREATH TECHNIQUE

1.  Place feet shoulder-distance apart.
2.  Stand with knees bent, as if you are about to sit on a raised stool. Your spine must be kept straight with your hands placed palms down on your lower abdomen.
3.  Exhale totally and begin diaphragmatic breathing; inhale through the nose.
4.  As you inhale, slowly raise your arms out to your sides, palms up, and inscribe as wide a circle as possible.
5.  At the same time, slowly straighten your knees so you are standing upright.
6.  Bring your palms together when your hands are overhead; make sure your lungs are full at the same time. Stretch from your ankles to the tips of your fingers.
7.  Hold the stretch for three breaths, and then release.
8.  Repeat the exercise three times.

*Beginner level.*

———————————○———————————

## HIP CIRCLES

11.2 ILLUSTRATION: HIP CIRCLES

*Purpose*

*To open and energize the pelvis.*

## HIP CIRCLES TECHNIQUE

1. Stand with feet shoulder-distance apart, knees bent, as if you were about to sit on a raised stool.

2. With your spine straight, place your hands on your hips.

3. Begin by rotating your hips to the right and then to the

left, leading with your pelvis as though you are dancing. Increase the amount of the turn each time.

4. Repeat until you have reached the maximum turn.

*Beginner level.*

---

# WINDMILLS

11.3 ILLUSTRATION: WINDMILLS

### Purpose

*To release tension in the body and allow energy to move upward.*

---

## WINDMILLS TECHNIQUE

1. Stand with feet shoulder-distance apart, knees bent as if you are about to sit on a raised stool.

2. With the spine and pelvis straight, begin swinging your arms from side to side across your body; allow your head to turn with your body and increase the length of the swing with each repetition. As you swing, let your arms gently hit your body.
3. Repeat several times.
*Beginner level.*

# WOOD CHOPPER

11.4 & 5 ILLUSTRATION: WOOD CHOPPER

**Purpose**
*Lessen fatigue in the upper back and open the chest.*

## WOOD CHOPPER TECHNIQUE

1. Stand with your feet shoulder-distance apart. Interlock fingers behind your back.

2. On an exhalation with knees slightly bent, fold forward at the waist and bring your arms forward, your fingers interlocked.

3. As you round your back, bring your chin toward your chest.

4. On inhalation, lift your chin away from your chest and arch your back, keeping your arms behind you.

5. Come to an upright position, unlock your fingers and bring your arms to your sides.

6. Repeat four to six times.

*Beginner through advanced level.*

# STANDING CAT/COW

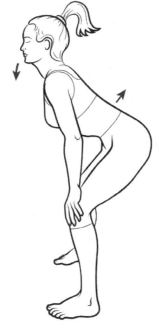

11.6 ILLUSTRATION: STANDING CAT/COW

## *Purpose*

*To create a flexible spine and release tension in the neck and shoulders.*

---

## STANDING CAT/COW TECHNIQUE

1. Stand with your feet shoulder-distance apart.
2. With knees slightly bent, bend over and bring your hands down to your knees.
3. With an exhalation, bring your chin toward your chest as you round your back.

4. On inhalation, lift your chin away from your chest and slowly arch your back.
5. Repeat, then let the right shoulder drop as you turn to look over your left shoulder.
6. Repeat, let the left shoulder drop as you look over your right shoulder.
7. Hold the positions as long as they seem comfortable.
8. With each repetition, extend the length of stretch.

*Beginner level.*

## ABDOMINAL SQUEEZE
### (Akunchana Prasarana)

11.7 ILLUSTRATION: ABDOMINAL SQUEEZE

*Purpose*

*To gain awareness and access to the abdominal and pelvic muscles in a standing pose.*

---○---

## ABDOMINAL SQUEEZE TECHNIQUE

1. Stand with your feet shoulder-distance apart.
2. Lean forward with the knees bent slightly. You may lean against the wall, buttocks touching, for stability.
3. Place the hands on the upper thighs where the arms can remain straight to support and rest the upper body.
4. Eyes can be opened or closed depending on your preference.
5. Tuck the chin to look at the naval or abdominal area.
6. Bring your awareness to the breath in the abdominal area.
7. Exhale, tilt the tailbone (coccyx) down, and contract the abdominal muscles toward the spine. Keep the upper body stable.
8. Inhale, lift the tailbone, and release the abdomen towards the floor as you feel the buttocks open and widen with the release. Again, here you can allow the pelvis to tilt with the contraction, and roll back on release. Think of the belly filling like a balloon.
9. Repeat five to seven times.

*Beginner level.*

---○---

**Note**: As you continue the practice over time, you can stabilize the pelvis so it doesn't move as you contract the pelvic floor, lower and upper abdomen. The pelvis should not rock as you release the upper and lower abdomen, and pelvic floor.

**Contraindications**: High blood pressure, glaucoma, heart disease.

## THE SQUAT

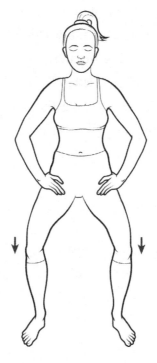

11.8 ILLUSTRATION: THE SQUAT

*Purpose*

*To strengthen the legs and buttocks.*

---

## THE SQUAT TECHNIQUE

1.  Stand with your feet slightly wider than shoulder-distance apart, toes out 10 to 25 degrees.
2.  Inhale as you bend your knees; slowly sink down as if about to sit on a stool.
3.  Keep your weight on your heels, thighs parallel to the floor, and knees aligned with your ankles, not your toes.
4.  Exhale and rise to a standing position. As you come up, draw the pubococcygeus muscle or PC muscle upward, as if you were drawing in energy from the earth. Then release. (The PC muscle extends from the pubic bone to the coccyx [tail bone] forming the floor of the pelvic cavity and supporting the pelvic organs.)
5.  Repeat three times.

*Beginner level.*

---

**Note**: When you are more advanced, you may hold weights in your hands, resting them on your thighs.

# THE LUNGE

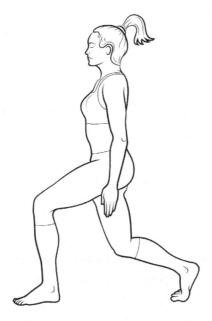

11.9 ILLUSTRATION: THE LUNGE

## Purpose

*To stretch and tone the pelvic region by enhancing the mobility of hip and groin muscles.*

---

## THE LUNGE TECHNIQUE

1. Stand with the feet shoulder-distance apart, arms down at your sides.
2. Maintaining balance, step forward with the left foot, enough to feel a stretch.
3. Keep weight on the heel of the left foot to keep pressure off the left knee.

4. On an inhalation, slowly lower your body until the left thigh is parallel to the floor.

5. Then exhale and come up slowly.

6. Repeat, switching sides each time.

*Beginner level.*

*Intermediates may add hand-held weights, increasing the weight.*

———————————————○———————————————

## LEG LIFTS

**Purpose**

*To specifically increase your metabolic vitality. Added benefits include toning the legs and stimulating the reproductive organs.*

———————————————○———————————————

### OVERALL LEG LIFTS TECHNIQUE

*All leg exercises will follow the same basic steps.*

1. Lie on your back. Before beginning leg exercises, support your back by resting on your elbows. (Absolute beginners can lie with their head down and hands wedged under the buttocks.) If you feel discomfort in your neck or lower back, adjust your position until there is no discomfort.

2. Begin each exercise by tucking your chin into your chest and inhaling as you lift your leg(s). You may lift one leg at a time or lift both legs at once.

3. As you lift each leg, be sure to extend it from your body, as if you were trying to elongate the leg muscles.

4.  While exhaling, lower the leg(s) and begin to lift your chin from your chest.
5.  Repeat eight to fifteen times, depending on your strength and endurance.

*Beginner level.*

## SINGLE STRAIGHT LIFTS

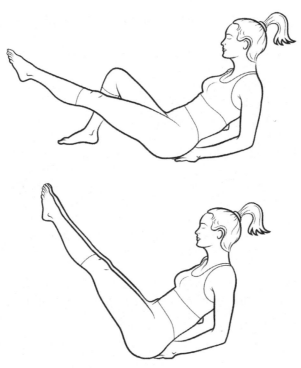

11.10 & 11 ILLUSTRATION: STRAIGHT LIFTS

**Note**: Follow Steps 1 to 5, starting with the left leg then going on to the right.

## DOUBLE LIFTS

**Note:** Follow Steps 1 to 5, raising both legs simultaneously. If you have discomfort in your lower back while lifting both legs, bend your knees until your abdominals get stronger. *Intermediate/advanced level.*

## PELVIC CIRCLE HIP RELEASER
(Adapted from Feldenkrais Method)[2]

11.12 ILLUSTRATION: PELVIC CIRCLE HIP RELEASER

*Purpose*
*To explore subtle movements of the pelvis; to gain access and channel the energy that resides there.*

## Pelvic Circle Hip Releaser Technique

1. Lie down on your back with your legs extended and your arms along your sides, palms facing the floor.

2. Bring your awareness to your breath and take a few moments to rest here. Spend a few minutes observing what thoughts are going through your mind, and notice how you feel physically.

3. As you inhale and exhale, notice which parts of your body move with the breath, and notice if one side of your body feels different than the other side. Pay particular attention to the way the back of your pelvis and the small of your back relate to the floor.

4. Bend both knees and place your feet on the floor, about hip-width distance apart. Imagine that the back of your pelvis is lying on a large, circular clock. The clock is oriented so that 12 o'clock is in the direction of your head and 6 o'clock is in the direction of your feet. The back of your pelvis is resting on the centre of the clock.

5. Start moving your pelvis gently and slowly between 12 o'clock and 6 o'clock. To move to 12 o'clock, flatten your lower back into the floor and slightly raise the tailbone. To move to 6 o'clock, increase the arch in the lower back and gently press the tailbone into the floor.

6. Repeat this movement a few times, paying attention to how the rest of your body responds.

7. Now start moving between 3 o'clock and 9 o'clock by tilting your pelvis a little to the left for 3 o'clock, and a little to

the right for 9 o'clock. Imagine where the numbers of the clock are as vividly as you can. Keep your knees pointing generally up toward the ceiling so that the movement is primarily in the hip joints. As you tilt your pelvis left and right, notice how your pelvis makes contact with the floor, and if the contact changes with your movements.

8.  After a short rest, continue the movement between 12 o'clock and 6 o'clock; still paying attention to how your pelvis moves.

9.  Spend a few minutes doing circles in a clockwise direction with your pelvis. Move very slowly and easily, attempting each time around to make the movement smoother and more circular. After a brief rest, try some circles in a counter-clockwise direction. Are different parts of the circle easier or more difficult when you are going in this direction?

10. Rest on your back and observe any changes in your relationship with the floor, particularly the back of your pelvis and your lower back. How are you breathing now? What is your emotional state, what are you thinking about?

11. Slowly roll onto your side, sit up, and then come to standing. Finally, walk around the room again and notice how your pelvis and your hips move as you walk.

*Beginner/Intermediate level.*

## METABOLIC MASTER I

11.13 & 14 ILLUSTRATION: METABOLIC MASTER I AND II

---

## METABOLIC MASTER I TECHNIQUE

1. From a supine position, rise and balance on your buttocks (hands underneath for balance if needed).

2. Bring your knees to your chest, toes pointed; keep your

head and neck steady.

3. Inhale; open your body like a flower, arms extended over your head, legs extended out.

4. Exhale, and lower your body to the floor.

5. Repeat three times.

*Intermediate level.*

---

## METABOLIC MASTER II TECHNIQUE

1. Lie flat on your back, arms overhead, legs extended, feet together.

2. Inhale, raise your lower and upper body until you roll onto your buttocks. Keep your back straight.

3. Hold for three seconds, then exhale and lower your body to the floor.

4. Repeat three times.

*Advanced Level.*

---

## METABOLISM CORE PRACTICES

The practices in this lesson continue to deepen our awareness of the abdominal region (hara), the place where we physically digest our food. This is also where we generate our core vitality and stamina. As we continue to work with the abdominal region, we begin to feel more strength and stability in our daily encounters. Our physical digestion also begins to show signs of strength and efficiency.

# PELVIC LIFT I

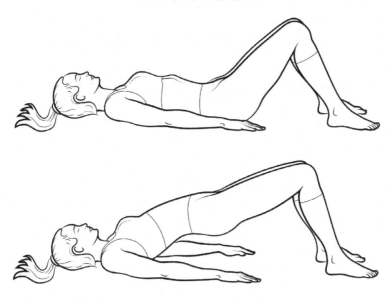

11.15 & 16 ILLUSTRATION: PELVIC LIFT I

## *Purpose*

*To gain awareness of the entire pelvic area from the base to the navel center. The pelvic/abdominal area holds all the digestive organs, as well as the associated emotions.*

## PELVIC LIFT I TECHNIQUE

1. Lie on your back, knees bent, feet flat on the floor, hip-distance apart, your hands extended down at your sides. It is better to have your feet closer than being set too far apart.

2. On inhalation, slowly roll up one vertebrae at a time, bringing the pelvis upward toward the ceiling. Keep your

shoulders and head flat on the floor, and do not use the arms for leverage.

3. Exhale, slowly bringing your body down to the starting position.

4. Repeat five times in unison with the breath.

*Beginner level.*

---

## PELVIC LIFT II

11.17 & 18 Illustration: Pelvic Lift II

**Purpose**

*Gain awareness of the pelvic floor and abdominal muscles.*

---○---

## PELVIC LIFT II TECHNIQUE

1. Sit on the floor with your knees bent, legs hip-width apart, feet flat on the floor. Place arms behind you, palms down on the floor, with fingers facing forward toward the heels.
2. Exhale and tilt chin toward chest.
3. Slowly inhale, untucking your chin as you lift your body and extend your pelvis toward the ceiling. Hold for as long as you are comfortable.
4. Repeat five times.

*Intermediate to advanced level.*

---○---

**Note**: To receive even more benefits from this pose add this version: while holding in position, keep the pelvis stationary, then contract the pelvic floor as well as the lower and upper abdomen. When you release, simply allow the belly to relax and fill. This will give an added dimension to the lift, making it deeper and wider.

## BRIDGE POSE

11.19 ILLUSTRATION: BRIDGE POSE

*Purpose:*

*To create space in the shoulders and chest area; strengthen your back, buttocks, and hamstrings; provide flexibility to your hips and thighs; increase flexibility and space between the vertebrae of your spine; calm your mind.*

## BRIDGE POSE TECHNIQUE

1. Lie on your back with your knees bent. Bring your feet directly under the knees, hip-width distance apart, heels directly under your knees. Rest your arms on the floor, palms flat.

2. Now, press your arms and shoulders into the floor; lift your pelvis. Lift the buttocks off the floor; extend your tailbone toward your heels.

3. As your chest rises, draw your shoulder blades toward each other and continue to lift onto your upper back. Clasp your hands and extend your arms along the floor beneath your

pelvis. Straighten your arms as much as possible, pressing your forearms into the floor. Work to keep the tops of your shoulders in alignment with the base of your neck.

5.  Now, rest the back of your head gently into the floor. Broaden through the collarbones and lift your chest up. Let your sternum move upward toward your chin.

6.  Practice three to four rounds of breathing while in the posture.

7.  To come out of the pose, release the interlaced fingers and with control slowly lower the torso to the floor.

8.  Repeat one to three times.

## SPHINX
### (Belly Down Back Bend)

11.20 ILLUSTRATION: SPHINX

### Purpose

*The Sphinx Pose helps to lengthen the abdominal muscles, strengthen the spine, and firm the buttocks. It also stretches and opens the chest, lungs, and shoulders. This pose invigorates the body and soothes the nervous system. It is also therapeutic for fatigue that results from expending too much energy, or from sitting too long.*

---

## SPHINX TECHNIQUE

1. Lie on your abdomen, elbows under your shoulders, forearms and hands flat on the floor, legs together.
2. Press the forearms down into the floor with elbows close to your sides and inhale, lift your head and chest off of the floor. Keep your neck in line with the spine.
3. Drop the shoulders down and back; press your chest forward. Draw your chin in towards the back of your neck. Look up toward your eyebrows.
4. Breathe and hold for two to six breaths.
5. To release: slowly lower your chest and head to the floor. Turn the head to one side, slide arms alongside your body and rest.
6. Repeat one to three times.

*Beginner level.*

---

# RECLINING TWIST

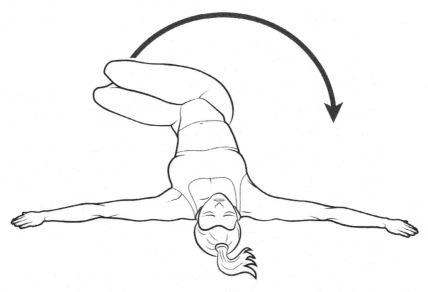

11.21 ILLUSTRATION: RECLINING TWIST

## *Purpose*

*To increase flexibility of the spine and relieve tension. You'll also be helping your metabolism by increasing blood flow to the digestive system.*

## RECLINING TWIST TECHNIQUE

1. Lie on your back and draw your knees to your chest.
2. Extend both arms out to the side.
3. Keep your shoulders on the floor and drop your knees to one side as you exhale. Hold for as long as you are comfortable.
4. Repeat on the other side.

5. Do this a minimum of three to four times. *Beginner level.*

---

**Note:** In a variation called the Pretzel Twist, the legs are intertwined. Let them fall to one side, then the other. This opens the pelvis. Intermediate level.

## SIX MINUTE REST AND RECOVER
### (Shavasana)

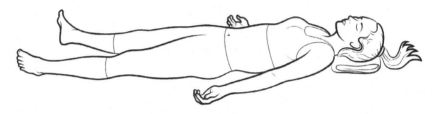

11.22 ILLUSTRATION: SHAVASANA

---

## SHAVASANA TECHNIQUE

1. Lie on the floor with a blanket beneath you and a pillow under your head. Place a bolster under your knees for support, if needed.
2. Bring your awareness to your breathing, your mind, and your body. Settle into the rhythm of your breath.
3. Relax and soften your forehead; relax your eyebrows and eyes; relax your nostrils. Exhale and inhale a few times. (Pause)

4. Relax your face, soften and relax the muscles of the neck..

5. Relax your shoulders, arms and fingertips. Breathe as though your breath is flowing all the way through your fingertips. (Pause)

6. Relax your chest, relax your heart region. Gently exhale and inhale. (Pause)

7. Relax your abdomen, pelvis, thighs, calves, feet and toes.

8. Breathe from the tips of your toes to the crown of your head, and the crown of your head to the tips of your toes. Breathe as though your breath is flowing through your whole body. (Pause)

9. Move your awareness back up through your toes, legs, through your lower back.

10. Bring your awareness to the mid and upper back, and release any residual tension that may be present. (Pause)

11. Bring your awareness to the back of your neck, the back of your head, and to the forehead. Rest your attention at the point above the eyebrow center, and pay attention to your breath.

12. Stay here as long as you like, taking care not to fall asleep. When finished, roll onto your left side for a few moments, then slowly rise to a seated position when you feel ready.

# CHAPTER 12

───────○───────

# The Healing Power of Meditation

*Meditation gives us access to the highest form of
the healing force and nourishment that
leads to self-transformation.*

I receive many calls when people feel overwhelmed and stressed hoping that yoga and meditation will help them. As someone who runs a home and a home business, and has struggled with finding quiet time in the midst of it all, I can relate to their dilemma.

Cheryl, a vibrant and kind woman, was the sister of one of my senior students. She worked from home, had three school-age children, and a six-year-old labrador retriever. She was a *tad* overwhelmed.

I suggested that she get up a bit earlier than the rest of her household in order to have some quiet, alone time. Rising this early would not be easy for her at first; it would require willpower and a desire to change a routine. To make early rising less challenging, I suggested that if she still felt tired after stretching and meditation time she should go back to bed and sleep a bit more. She agreed to try this.

After a month of rising at 5am, Cheryl reported back.

"I have to say, this feels like some magic formula! In the past I would just spin out of bed, let the dog out, get the kids ready for school, and then rush to be online for my business. Susan, I cannot believe what a difference just taking thirty minutes of 'me time' has made. You know, exercising, and meditating before I jump into my day, has changed everything for me. I feel like I have more control over my life and my health."

Most people are surprised to find that they don't want to go back to bed after meditation practice. Enjoying the quiet time of meditation gives us a deep quality of rest, so we have less need for that little bit of extra sleep. The American Institute of Stress reports that more than 75-90% of doctor visits are related to stress and fatigue.[1] When I first heard this statistic, I was stunned—75% or more? Upon reflection, though, it really isn't so surprising. After all who can question that as the pace of life accelerates, there is an increasing amount of stress we are facing in our world? Just a few years ago, phone messages, emails, and news updates were things we could walk away from; now they're in our pockets or handbags at all times. Many of us face health care costs—or a lack of medical insurance—that create a constant hum of worry and uncertainty in the backs of our minds. What also contributes to stress is the knowledge that today our financial security in retirement is far from secure.

At one time, only physicians and emergency personnel were on call around the clock; now it seems as if we all are. In order to be competitive in our workplaces—and keep our jobs—we have to stay at pace with the ever changing technological innovations. Our kids also seem to enter their own kind of competitive environment early in their lives, especially when they are carrying a schedule packed with extracurricular activities and schedules.

As we adapt to these exceptionally challenging times, most of us are struggling, to one extent or another. We are living with fatigue, anxiety, stress, depression, and sleep problems. Stress-related health issues, ranging from attention deficit disorder to depression, heart disease, and anxiety disorders, are on the rise. Around the world there has been a massive increase in the incidence of mental health problems, especially among young people. Suicide, violence, and depression are also on the rise, according to the World Health Organization. Mental health issues are fast becoming the number one health concern this century, with one in four people suffering in a given year. This figure translates to 57.7 million people.[2] Paradoxically, in a nation of abundance, we are experiencing malnutrition on every level: physical, emotional, mental, and spiritual.

- Major depression affects approximately 15 million American adults, affecting more women than men.[2]
- Major depressive disorder is the leading cause of disability in the U.S. for ages 15-44.[2]
- Anxiety disorders afflict 40 million American adults aged 18 to 54.[2]

- Panic disorder affects the health of 6 million Americans in the same age bracket.[2]
- Alzheimer's Disease affects more than 5 million Americans. The number of Americans with AD has more than doubled since 1980.[3]

The average person today suffers from fatigue, and unhappiness, that stems from a lack of vitality and an agitated mind. Our peace of mind, it seems, has been lost, along with much of our creativity, productivity, and general health. The losses we suffer because of our hyper-culture affect us on the deepest level. The more that life demands we are energetic, the more real-life energy we lose. Vital energy—our life force—is being consumed each day with every shortcut or speedup.

What is going on, and what is going wrong? How can we stay mentally sharp and even happy in these hectic times? As you participate in this "new normal" daily life, perhaps now is the time to create your strategy to get off the stress rollercoaster.

The solution certainly doesn't lie solely in modern medicine's pharmaceutical practices. "Better living through chemistry" simply has not been working for everyone. The traditional allopathic medical model does not fully concern itself with its effects on our being, or our healing energy. In a short time, our physical-psychological energy matrix becomes unbalanced through the use of these drugs.

Many of us are afflicted with energetic blockages and inertia. Life is a complex interrelationship of forces, and to understand it we must examine the anatomy of who we are.

————○————

In traditional cultures throughout history, the mind and body have been viewed as inseparable parts of us. Meditation has been one of the tools used by these cultures to access the energy of the mind, body, and spirit, and to cultivate greater awareness. For thousands of years in the East, meditation has been a traditional practice.

In the 1960's meditation became more accessible to the West within the context of science. At that time scientists studied the practice of meditation and its effects on the human mind and body. Researchers began recording changes in the practitioners' physical functions: blood pressure, heart rate, respiratory function, and production of stress hormones.

In the Western world of the early 1970's, meditation was often touted as a relaxation technique for alleviating physical stress. Although the concept of a "relaxation response" was convenient as an initial explanation for what was happening in the meditative state, later work showed that physiologically it was much more complex than a decrease in heart and respiratory rate. Thankfully, by the 1990's, meditation was becoming accepted as a *medicine* to support healing, and was integrated with stress-reduction programs offered at many traditional health care facilities. One well-known example is the Mindfulness Based Stress Reduction (MBSR) Clinic, founded by Jon Kabat-Zinn, PhD, at the University of Massachusetts Medical Center. Their early research found that mental discipline and meditative practices can change the workings of the brain, and open the door to different levels of awareness.[4]

Today, ancient healing traditions and modern medicine alike recognize meditation and stress reduction techniques as a proven approach for restoring balance and vitality to the overstressed body and mind.

―――――○―――――

The growing popularity of yoga has offered many people a glimpse into the benefits of meditation. Yoga postures are traditionally intended as a preparation for deeper meditative experiences, yet many yoga classes address only the physical aspects of the practice. The meditation practice I teach in this program will do for your mind what yoga does for your body. It will relax the mind's "muscle," create more mental flexibility, and help build resilience. The mind will become fit and more adaptable to the situations we meet in everyday life. Stress will no longer be something that comes in unannounced to create havoc. You will find your unique point of balance.

The Healing Power of Meditation course I teach is based on traditional yoga meditation developed over thousands of years, and it draws on time tested practices rooted in Yoga Science. You will learn to connect to your radiance—the source of sustainable energy that positively influences the mind, body, and senses. You will learn to become calm and steady. Regular practice will build the inner strength and focus you need for a balanced life. One of the best and most accessible books on authentic meditation is *Vishoka Meditation: The Yoga of Inner Radiance.*[5] This is a must read for anyone who is interested in learning about meditation.

―――――○―――――

We tend to search outside of ourselves for answers, when in fact, the answers to our questions, and the source of healing is inside of us. We often do so, because as a culture, our spiritual understanding has not developed along with our advances in technology. Though many new inventions assist us in living, these same inventions cannot show us the way to live a healthy, illumined life. As a society, our attention to the spiritual aspect of our being is essential to prevent our technological "progress" from becoming a destructive force.

Spirituality is recognition of the life force that lies inside of us. We must have radiance and vitality as the foundation for our abundance and development, if we are to evolve and mature . . . indeed, if we are to survive at all. There's only one way out, and that is in. It is where our inner luminosity resides.

Viewing both Eastern and Western disciplines as a part of the big picture allows us to have a more holistic view of healing and self discovery in the modern world. The vision offered through this approach is what we need to live in this hyperculture, while at the same time connecting with the inner core of our being. We term this "holistic medicine" or "mind-body medicine."

We can begin our journey to health only by acknowledging and honoring the dynamic interconnectedness of our exquisitely designed human system. Meditation teaches us that simple breath and simple posture is key to being aware of these connections. In this profound, ancient form of restorative therapy, your greatest counsel comes while sitting on your cushion. As you will see, meditation practice allows you to travel inward, ultimately guiding your awareness toward self-healing.

## FOCUSED AWARENESS

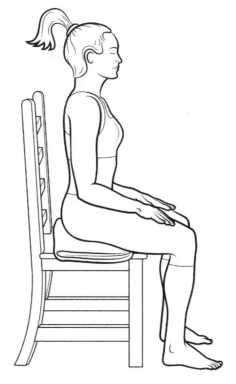

11.23 ILLUSTRATION: FOCUSED AWARENESS

### Goal

Pave the way for the Healing Power of Meditation.

### Practice

A beginning meditation

### Exercise

Choose a time each day when you will not be interrupted. Start with just ten minutes in the beginning, then you can add to your time over the course of several weeks. Mornings or evenings are the most preferred times. It's easiest to form the habit of meditation either first thing in the morning or just before retiring in the evening. Turn off the phone and find a quiet space. Sit quietly and comfortably with your eyes closed and your head, neck, and spine in a straight line. Practice alternate-nostril breathing for one round.

Remain sitting; follow the flow of breath in and out of both your nostrils. Continue this for the next three to five minutes as you allow thoughts and feelings to come forward. As these impressions arise, just observe them as if you were watching a movie. Keep focusing on your breath with the intention of releasing all your tension and fatigue. Allow your body and mind to rest in this space for a few moments.

Now take time to reflect on the areas of your body calling out to you for healing. Focus; now breathe into that space. Imagine filling these places in your body with the freshness and vital force of your breath. Embrace the thought of wellness for your whole being.

When you are ready to come out of meditation, place your palms over your eyes and gently open your eyes. Rest your hands on your thighs and continue to enjoy the stillness.

## MEDITATION IS A PRACTICE

Meditation is a practice and a process. It is an experience that unfolds your awareness gradually. It is not listening with a headset to different tones and pitches, seeing visions, or for that matter, anything that implies an instant method. I remember someone saying to me that they had achieved a state of meditation with a computer program. They indicated that their experience of one week with this program was equivalent to twenty years of meditation. This is nonsense and don't believe it. In our culture, people expect results to happen without putting forth much effort. To practice meditation requires a commitment to learning, and a lifestyle that supports the practice. You cannot cultivate a garden instantly, just as you cannot magically create a meditation practice. Cultivation requires time.

Rules of the path:
1.  Be vigilant when it comes to practice. Choose a clean, quiet and well-ventilated space, free of distractions.
2.  Do not expect immediate results. Ask yourself this: how long did it take to learn how to read, or play an instrument, or learn a new job?
3.  Don't let progress get side tracked with your imagination.

If you find yourself saying, "I don't have time to meditate," then stop and be aware that you are not making meditation a priority. If you find yourself saying "meditation is not so easy," then you are off to a good start.

# SCIENCE IS PRECISION

*Meditation is a technique that needs to be taught in a systematic way, with precision.* This is the way that I was taught. If you learn how to systematically practice meditation, it will not take much time for you to see some progress, provided you know the full technique. Some teachers extract one small aspect of an ancient practice and then say they are teaching meditation. This is not authentic instruction of meditation and it causes dissatisfaction. You need to approach meditation with full intention, because it is easy to get discouraged in the beginning and drop the practice.

Here are some pointers to establishing and refining your meditation practice:

1. It is important to maintain your desire to meditate. Realize that you will need to stay committed and be focused, because meditation requires that you discipline your mind. It may not always be so easy.

2. When you make the commitment to sit each day, decide that you will not let anything get in the way.

Sri Swami Rama once said:

*Don't meditate if you are not inclined to meditate. If you want to meditate, you have to form a habit, because habit weaves your character and personality. If you really want to know who you are, you have to take off all the masks, one after the other. If you are prepared to do that, you can learn to tread the path of meditation.*

SRI SWAMI RAMA LECTURE, HIMALAYAN INSTITUTE, 1995

3. Finally, simply sit in meditation, don't try to see lights, images, or colors. Learn to sit still. Meditation begins in stillness.

Now is the time for each and every one of us to learn to meditate in order to ride the waves of our tumultuous modern society. Meditation gives us access to the highest form of the healing force and nourishment that leads to self-transformation.

# Return to Radiance

PART IV

---○---

# The Start-up 21 Day Plan

# NOTES ON THE DIET PLAN

- Desserts are not included in the menus but are optional at lunch.
- An asterisk denotes that the recipe is included in the recipe section.
- Preferably, all food should be eaten before 7 p.m.
- Breakfast should be eaten before 8 a.m.
- Meals are suggestions, feel free to substitute meals, or repeat meals that you enjoy. Keep in mind, lunches are the big meal of the day for optimal digestion. Dinner meals are lighter, to support balance and to assure complete digestion. The goal is to establish complete metabolic balance.
- Consult your health care provider before conducting an overnight fast or eliminating dairy products entirely from your diet.

# MENU AND DIET PLAN

## - DAY 1 -

**UPON ARISING**
Morning Rejuvenator*

**BREAKFAST**
Metabolic Cleanser*
Oat Cereal with Flaxseed and Almond Milk* (optional)

**LUNCH**
Baked Falafel*
Steamed Green Beans
Whole Grain Bread with Topping
Beverage
Dessert (optional)

**DINNER**
Miso Soup
Gingered Fish
Mixed Steamed Greens*
Warm beverage

## - DAY 2 -

**UPON ARISING**
Morning Rejuvenator*

**BREAKFAST**
Hormone Balancer*
Rice Cereal with Almond Milk* (optional)

**LUNCH**
Grilled Chicken Sandwich or Hummus Wrap
Wild-Rice Salad*
Beverage
Dessert (Optional)

**DINNER**
Vegetarian burger
Roasted Rice*
Broccoli with Olive Oil and Lemon
Warm beverage

## - DAY 3 -

**UPON ARISING**
Morning Rejuvenator*

## BREAKFAST
Fresh Fruit Plate with Granola Topping*
Toasted Oats* (Optional)

## LUNCH
Pizza Linguine Style*
Energy Salad with Olive Oil/Garlic or Classic Vinaigrette
    Dressing*
Beverage
Dessert (optional)

## DINNER
Black Bean Soup
Steamed Garlic Broccoli
Warm Beverage

## - DAY 4 -

## UPON ARISING
Morning Rejuvenator*

## BREAKFAST
Vitality Promoter*
Blueberry Bran Muffin (optional)

## LUNCH

Phytoestrogen Delight*

Whole Grain Toasted Bread

Fresh Fruit

Beverage

Dessert (optional)

## DINNER

Broiled Wild Caught Salmon with Lemon

Steamed rice

Energy Salad*

Warm beverage

## - DAY 5 -

## UPON ARISING

Morning Rejuvenator*

## BREAKFAST

Fresh Grapefruit Juice

Muesli Cereal with Almond Milk (optional)

## LUNCH

Pasta Pesto*

Whole Grain Muffin with Fruit Spread

Beverage

Dessert (optional)

**DINNER**

Mineral Mountain*

Stuffed Zucchini*

Green Salad with Olive Oil Vinaigrette

Warm Beverage

## - DAY 6 -

**UPON ARISING**

Morning Rejuvenator*

**BREAKFAST**

Banana Berry Protein Shake*

Sweet Fruit Salad* (optional)

Toasted English Muffin with Butter

**LUNCH**

Vegetable Bean Pie* *or*

Sprouted Rye Bread with Hummus Spread*

Beverage

Dessert (optional)

**DINNER**

Thyroid Balancer (kelp soup)*

Baked Turkey Breast or Tempeh

Sautéed Vegetables

Baked Yam

Warm Beverage

## - DAY 7 -

### UPON ARISING
Morning Rejuvenator*

### BREAKFAST
Mixed Organic Berries
Toasted Oatmeal with Almond Milk and Raisins* (optional)

### LUNCH
Fatigue Eliminator*
Lentil Soup*
Energy Salad*
Beverage
Dessert (optional)

### DINNER
Broiled Scallops with Lemon
Asparagus with Honey-Lemon Dressing*
Scalloped Potatoes with Greens
Warm Beverage

## - DAY 8 -

### UPON ARISING
Morning Rejuvenator*

**BREAKFAST**

Fresh Vegetable or Fruit Juice

Egg White Omelet with Peppers and Onions (optional)

**LUNCH**

Stuffed Eggplant*

Steamed Collard Greens with Olive Oil and Lemon

Beverage

Dessert (optional)

**DINNER**

Tempeh, Mushrooms, and Snow Peas on a Bed of Rice*

Green Salad

Warm Beverage

## - DAY 9 -

**UPON ARISING**

Morning Rejuvenator*

**BREAKFAST**

Fresh Fruit

Dry Cereal with Berries and Almond Milk (optional)

**LUNCH**

Pasta and Tomato Pesto Sauce with Cheese*

Arugula Salad with Balsamic Vinegar

Beverage

Dessert (optional)

**DINNER**

Poached Wild-Salmon or Lentil Salad

Garlicky Greens*

Fruit Sorbet

Warm Beverage

## - DAY 10 -

**UPON ARISING**

Morning Rejuvenator*

**BREAKFAST**

Vitality Promoter*

Toasted Oatmeal, with Almond or Oat Milk, Raisins and Spices (optional)

**LUNCH**

Tabouleh*

Energy Salad*

Beverage

Dessert (optional)

**DINNER**

Marinated Organic Tempeh*

Steamed greens

Warm beverage

## - DAY 11 -

**UPON ARISING**

Morning Rejuvenator*

**BREAKFAST**

Grapefruit Juice

Whole Grain Muffin with Apple Butter (optional)

**LUNCH**

Tuna melt

Sea Vegetable Salad*

Beverage

Dessert (optional)

**DINNER**

Baked Turkey Breast or Sautéed Tempeh

Herbed Rice

Broccoli Spears with Lemon

Warm Beverage

## - DAY 12 -

**UPON ARISING**
Morning Rejuvenator*

**BREAKFAST**
Metabolic Cleanser*
Stewed Prunes with Whole Grain Muffin (optional)

**LUNCH**
Swiss Chard Pan Pizza*
Grated Carrot Salad with Raisins, and Yogurt
Beverage
Dessert (optional)

**DINNER**
Grilled Zucchini Drizzled with Olive Oil
Chickpeas in Tomato/Basil Fennel Sauce*
Wild Rice Salad
Warm Beverage

## - DAY 13 -

**UPON ARISING**
Morning Rejuvenator*

**BREAKFAST**

Fruit Smoothie*

Baked Muffin with Apple Butter (optional)

**LUNCH**

Lentil Salad in Pita Bread

Fruit Sorbet

Beverage

**DINNER**

Poached Cod with Tomato, Parsely, and Garlic

Veggie Burger

Sautéed Greens

Seasoned Rice

Warm Beverage

## - DAY 14 -

**UPON ARISING**

Morning Rejuvenator*

**BREAKFAST**

Vitality Promoter*

Eggless Organic Tofu* with Whole Grain Bread and Almond Butter (optional)

## LUNCH

Vegetable Bean Soup

Whole Grain Bread

Beverage

Dessert (optional)

## DINNER

Ratatouille Over Rice* or

Cucumber Tomato Salad with Chickpeas and Vinaigrette*

Warm Beverage

## - DAY 15 -

## UPON ARISING

Morning Rejuvenator*

## BREAKFAST

Fruit Smoothie*

Egg-White Omelet with Mushrooms and Spinach* (optional)

## LUNCH

Soup of Choice

Spinach Salad with Whole Grain Roll

Beverage

Dessert (optional)

**DINNER**
Baked Fish and Fresh Herbs
Sautéed Brussels Sprouts*
Hummus Wrap
Warm Beverage

## - DAY 16 -

**UPON ARISING**
Morning Rejuvenator*

**BREAKFAST**
Vegetable-Apple Juice Cocktail*
Zucchini Bread* (optional)

**LUNCH**
Cold Pasta Salad with Tomato, Basil and Flaked Cod*(or Tempeh)
Energy Salad*
Beverage
Dessert (optional)

**DINNER**
Protein Burger
Grilled Vegetables
Pineapple Wedges

## - DAY 17 -

**UPON ARISING**

Morning Rejuvenator*

**BREAKFAST**

Fruit or Juice

Granola with Almond Milk (optional)

**LUNCH**

Tofu Chickenless Salad*

Whole Grain Toast

Beverage

Dessert (optional)

**DINNER**

Curried Beans

Stir-fried Greens with Ginger*

Fresh Fruit

Warm Beverage

## - DAY 18 -

**UPON ARISING**

Morning Rejuvenator*

**BREAKFAST**

Fresh Fruit

Toasted Oatmeal* with Soy, Almond or Oat Milk and Banana (optional)

**LUNCH**

Garden Burger*

Endive Salad

Beverage

Dessert (optional)

**DINNER**

Marinated Shrimp and Chicken Kabobs with Grilled Vegetables*

Herbed Rice

Chickpeas with Tomato Sauce

Warm Beverage

## - DAY 19 -

**UPON ARISING**

Morning Rejuvenator*

**BREAKFAST**

Apple juice

Toasted Whole Grain Bread with Sesame Butter (optional)

**LUNCH**

Whole Grain Falafel Sandwich with Onion and Tomato

Light Vegetable Soup*

Beverage

Dessert (optional)

**DINNER**

Mineral Mountain*

Tempeh Vegetable Stir-fry*

Warm Beverage

## - DAY 20 -

**UPON ARISING**

Morning Rejuvenator*

**BREAKFAST**

Vitality Promoter*

Dry Cereal with Berries

**LUNCH**

Couscous Salad (alternative: Quinoa Tabbouleh Salad)*

Tomato Soup

Beverage

Dessert (optional)

**DINNER**

Rosemary Chicken

Mixed Steamed Greens

Rice Pilaf

Grilled Tofu or Tempeh

Warm Beverage

## - DAY 21 -

**UPON ARISING**

Morning Rejuvenator*

**BREAKFAST**

Hormone Balancer*

Whole Grain Muffin with Fruit Jam (optional)

**LUNCH**

Vegetable Stir-Fry on Rice with Shrimp and Tempeh

Beverage

Dessert (optional)

**DINNER**

Grilled Root Vegetables with Aduki Beans

Sautéed Greens with Sesame Seeds*

Warm Beverage

## RECOMMENDED BEVERAGES

| | |
|---|---|
| Green tea | Rice milk |
| Herb teas | Coffee substitutes |
| Kukicha Tea | Organic coffee |
| Fresh, fruit & vegetable juices | Organic milk |
| Water | Raw milk |
| Almond milk | |

## RECIPES FOR THE VITALITY DIET

**Note**: You may make substitutions in all recipes—for example, use grapefruit juice instead of lemon juice. For ease, you can use precooked organic beans, and frozen fruits and vegetables as substitutes for fresh foods, but use canned foods sparingly. Many of the dishes are available at salad bars and restaurants. Vegetarian alternatives in this plan can be used as a substitute for any of the non-vegetarian meals. Salt has not been added to the recipes, use your own discretion about the amount that works best for you. I want to emphasize that you follow the basic format and eat as many healthy foods as possible.

---------------------------- **DAY 1** ----------------------------

### Morning Rejuvenator

Juice of ½ large lemon (or 1 small)

4-6 oz. spring water (room temperature or heated)

1-2 tsp. honey or unsulfured blackstrap molasses

1. Combine ingredients and drink.
2. Alternative: Use half the amount of lemon juice and add a pinch of cayenne pepper.

### Metabolic Cleanser

Juice of ½ medium grapefruit

Juice of 1 medium orange

1 tsp. lemon juice

¼ cup frozen blueberries or 1 banana

1. Combine ingredients in a blender for 15 seconds and serve.

### Oat Cereal with Flaxseed and Almond Milk* (optional)

⅓ cup rolled oats (not quick oats)

1 cup water

1 tsp. ground flaxseed

⅓ cup berries or cut fruit

almond milk

1. Place oats in warm iron skillet and keep stirring over medium heat until golden brown.

2. Remove oats from skillet and place in medium saucepan with water. Bring to a boil over high heat.
3. Reduce heat to low. Cover and cook until desired consistency, 5-7 minutes.
4. Add flaxseed and let stand for 3 minutes.
5. Add almond milk, fruit and serve.


**Baked Falafel**

4 cups dried chickpeas that have been soaked overnight in 3 cups water, drained

2 tsp. cumin

1 tsp. turmeric

1 tsp. sea salt

6 scallions, minced

¼ cup water

1 tbsp. lemon juice

1 tbsp. olive oil

½ cup organic flour


1. Preheat oven to 350 degrees.
2. Coat a baking sheet with olive oil and heat in oven for 10 minutes.
3. Place all ingredients except flour in food processor and combine at medium speed for 10 seconds.
4. Form mixture into patties about 3 ½ inches in diameter and 2/3 inch thick.
5. Coat patties lightly with flour and place on hot baking sheet. Bake for 10 minutes on each side.

### Mixed Steamed Greens

2 lbs. Russian Kale (curly kale or purple kale)

2 lbs. collard greens

2 lbs. Swiss chard

1 tbsp. olive oil

3-4 cloves garlic, chopped

1 leek, chopped

½ cup water

1. Wash all the greens. Do not dry. Chop fine.
2. Heat large skillet or wok over medium heat.
3. Add oil, sauté garlic and leek.
4. Add greens and toss. Sprinkle greens with just enough water to keep from sticking to the pot. Cover and cook on low heat until the greens are tender, 3-5 minutes.
5. Remove from heat, and let sit for 5 minutes in covered pot. Serve.

## DAY 2

### Hormone Balancer

1 cup vanilla almond milk

1-2 tbsp. protein powder

½ frozen banana

Juice of 2 oranges or 1 cup berries

1. Combine ingredients in a blender for 15 seconds. Serve cold.

**Rice Cereal with Almond Milk** (An alternative to oatmeal)

1 cup cooked basmati rice

¼-½ tsp. cinnamon

¼ cup minced ginger (optional)

1 cup almond milk

2 tbsp. local honey or maple syrup

1. Put rice, cinnamon, ginger (if desired) and almond milk in small saucepan and mix well.
2. Cook over medium heat, about 5 minutes.
3. Add honey (or maple syrup) and serve.

### Wild Rice Salad

½ cup wild rice with ¼ cup brown rice (any variety)

2 cups pre-packaged vegetable stock

1-2 cups chopped kale and/or spinach

2 scallions, chopped

1. Put the rice in a stock pot, rinse. Add the vegetable stock and bring to a boil. Reduce the heat to the lowest setting. Cook for 50-60 minutes.
2. Add greens and scallions putting them on top of the rice (do not stir),
3. For the last 15 minutes of cooking time. Serve immediately.

### Roasted Rice

1 cup long- grain brown rice

2 cups water or vegetarian vegetable stock

Pinch of sea salt (optional)

1. Put rice in iron skillet over medium heat. Stir until kernels are lightly browned.
2. Remove rice from skillet and place in medium saucepan with water or stock and salt. Bring to a boil and cover.
3. Reduce heat to medium low and simmer until water is absorbed 50-60 minutes.
4. Remove from heat and let stand for 5-10 minutes, covered.
5. Remove the lid and serve.

## DAY 3

### Fresh Fruit Plate with Granola Topping
½ pineapple, cubed
1-2 kiwis
1 banana
¼ cup granola (see below)

1. Cut fruits into bite-sized pieces. Add granola topping and serve.

### Granola
4-5 cups oats (avoid quick oats)
1 cup sweetener ( maple syrup, molasses)
¼ cup chopped pecans
¼ cup sunflower seeds
½ cup chopped dates (optional)

2 tbsp. flaxseeds (optional)

1. Preheat oven to 300 degrees.
2. Mix all ingredients and put on baking sheet.
3. Cook until golden brown or to the dryness you like, stirring every 5 minutes. Let cool.
4. Store in tight jar and refrigerate

## Toasted Oats

⅓ cup rolled oats
1 cup water, or milk
1/8 tsp. cinnamon
Pinch of ginger powder(optional)
Ghee, honey or maple sugar (optional)

1. Place the oats in a warm iron skillet and toast over medium heat until golden brown.
2. Remove oats from skillet and place in medium saucepan with milk or water. Bring to a boil.
3. Reduce heat to low. Add cinnamon and ginger. Cook until desired consistency, 5-10 minutes. Add ghee, honey, or maple sugar to taste.

## Pizza Linguine Style

½ chopped onion
2-3 cloves garlic
1 tbsp. fennel seeds
1 tbsp. olive oil

1 cup chopped mushrooms

½ cup chopped eggplant

½ chopped zucchini

1½ cups tomato sauce (use your favorite fat-free, sugar-free variety)

½-1 cup cubed organic tofu

1 tbsp. oregano

8-10 oz. pasta

1. Preheat oven to 375 degrees.
2. Sauté onions, garlic, and fennel seeds in olive oil. Set aside.
3. Combine the rest of the ingredients (except pasta) in a medium saucepan and simmer for 15-20 minutes over low heat.
4. Cook pasta in separate pot. Drain and put in casserole dish.
5. Add vegetable mixture on top of pasta. Bake for 25 minutes.

**Energy Salad**

3 cups romaine lettuce, or other leaf lettuce, such as radicchio, watercress, or Boston

1-2 organic tomatoes, sliced

1 carrot, sliced

1 cucumber, sliced

1. Combine ingredients and serve with one of the dressings below.

### Olive Oil/Garlic Dressing

1 tbsp. olive oil

2 cloves garlic, minced

Juice of ½ lemon

Pinch of cayenne pepper (optional)

1. Combine ingredients in jar and shake vigorously.

### Classic Vinaigrette Dressing

1 tbsp. olive oil or other oil, such as Macadamia,
    sesame or walnut

2 tbsp. vinegar

1. Combine in jar and shake vigorously.

**Note**: For variety, add minced garlic, mustard, fresh herbs such as basil, honey or brown rice syrup. Experiment for yourself.

## DAY 4

### Vitality Promoter

4 large carrots

1 large red beet (or 2 medium)

2 stalks celery

10 parsley or cilantro sprigs

2 collard green, or kale leaves

Juice of 1 lemon

1.  Place carrots, beets, celery, parsley and greens in a juicer.
2.  Add the lemon juice.
3.  Mix and serve.

### Phytoestrogen Delight

½ lb. organic-non GMO tofu, cubed

1 tsp. Turmeric powder

1 tsp. Mustard powder

Protein powder (optional)

½ green pepper, chopped

1 scallion, chopped

1.  In a food processor or bowl add tofu, turmeric, mustard and protein powder.
2.  Blend well for 10 seconds.
3.  Hand-mix in green pepper and scallion.
4.  Serve alone or on toast.

## DAY 5

### Pasta Pesto

2-3 cups basil leaves, washed and dried

¾ cup olive oil

1 tsp. Fine sea salt

1 tbsp. lemon juice (optional)

½ cup grated Parmesan cheese (optional)

Freshly ground black pepper

¼ cup toasted whole pine nuts (use unsalted pistachio nuts for lower fat-substitute)

1. Combine all ingredients except pine nuts in food processor. Blend for 15 seconds.
2. Transfer to a bowl, add pine nuts and stir.
3. Refrigerate before serving. For later use, store in freezer.

### Mineral Mountain

1 qt. water

1 cup wakame seaweed

1 cup cubed organic-non-GMO tofu

1 tbsp. shredded kombu seaweed

1 scallion, chopped

1-2 tbsp. miso paste

Wheat free tamari to taste (optional)

1. In saucepan, combine all ingredients except miso paste and tamari.
2. Bring to a boil and let simmer for 10 minutes.
3. In separate cup put miso and add ¼ - ½ cup of soup mixture to dissolve. Let stand for 5 minutes.
4. Add miso mixture to saucepan.
5. Add tamari to taste and stir, serve.

## Stuffed Zucchini

4 medium zucchini

1 tbsp. olive oil

1 small onion, chopped

1 beaten egg or 2 beaten egg whites

1 cup chopped organic-non-GMO tofu, feta or goat cheese

¼ tsp. cayenne pepper

1 dash nutmeg

1 tsp. unrefined sea salt

½ cup whole-grain bread crumbs

¼ tsp. sweet paprika

1. Preheat oven to 350 degrees.
2. Cut zucchini lengthwise. Scoop out the inside of the zucchini and chop, leaving the shell of the zucchini for later. Place chopped zucchini in medium-sized bowl.
3. In skillet, heat olive oil and sauté onion until soft. Add to the bowl with the chopped zucchini.
4. In the same skillet, sauté zucchini shells on both sides over medium heat until lightly brown.
5. Add beaten egg, tofu or cheese, cayenne, nutmeg, salt and bread crumbs to onion mixture. Mix thoroughly.
6. Divide stuffing among eight shells.
7. Bake for 20-25 minutes.

## DAY 6

### Banana Berry Protein Shake

1-2 frozen bananas

½ cup organic strawberries or other berries in season

2 cups vanilla almond or oat milk

1. Combine fruit in a bowl. Mix honey and almonds and dribble on top.

### Vegetable Bean Pie

2-3 tbsp. water

2 large tomatoes, sliced

2 zucchini, cubed

1 cup sliced mushrooms

½-1 cup grated cheese or cheese alternative

1 onion, finely chopped

2-3 cloves garlic, finely chopped

1 cup vegetable broth (reconstituted from a powder)

½ cup uncooked brown rice

3 eggs whites, well blended

1-2 cups cooked garbanzo beans (chickpeas), rinsed and drained

1 tsp. olive oil

1. Pour vegetable broth into a saucepan. Add rinsed rice and bring to a boil. Then lower heat and cook on low until water is absorbed. 50-60 minutes.

2. Preheat oven to 350 degrees.

3. Put water in another saucepan, add tomatoes, zucchini, mushrooms, onion and garlic. Bring to a boil, reduce heat to low and steam approximately 5 minutes. Uncover and let stand.

4. Combine egg whites, beans and basil and stir into the rice.

5. Cover bottom of a baking dish with olive oil to prevent sticking and then spread the rice mixture.

6. Spread the vegetables over the rice, and sprinkle cheese on top. Bake 50-60 minutes.

### Hummus Spread

2 cups cooked chickpeas

⅔ (approximately) cup bean liquid

2 tbsp. lemon juice

2 scallions, chopped (optional)

2-3 cloves garlic

3 tbsp. tahini (sesame butter)

½ tsp. sea salt

1. Soak one cup of dry chickpeas overnight, drain.

2. Simmer the chickpeas on low heat in a slightly open, covered pot with 5 cups of water. Check every 20-30 minutes, you may need to add more water. Cook for 3-4 hours or until they mash easily between your fingers. Drain well and save liquid.

3. Put the beans, lemon juice, scallions and garlic in a blender or food processor with just enough liquid from the beans to blend.
4. Add the tahini and salt and mix well. Note: Tahini will thicken the mixture, so adjust the consistency with additional liquid from the beans.

**Thyroid Balancer** (Kelp Soup)

4 cups water
6-inch piece of kombu (kelp) seaweed
2 carrots, finely chopped
1 cup collard greens, finely chopped
Miso
Tamari (optional)

1. Soak the kombu (kelp) in warm water for 30 minutes. Drain and add fresh water, cook on low for 20 minutes. Drain and cool. Cut into ½ inch squares and set aside.
2. In a saucepan, combine all ingredients except kelp, miso, and tamari.
3. Bring to a boil and let simmer for 10 minutes.
4. In a separate cup, put miso and dissolve with ¼-½ cup of soup mixture. Let stand for 5 minutes.
5. Turn off heat under the saucepan.
6. Add miso mixture and kombu pieces to the saucepan. Let stand for 5 minutes.
7. Add tamari to taste and serve.

## DAY 7

### Fatigue Eliminator

7 sprigs of parsley

1 cucumber

1 large red beet or two medium beets

4 large carrots

Juice of ½-1 lemon

Cayenne pepper (optional)

1. In a blender juicer, add parsley and cucumber, followed by beets and carrots.
2. Add the lemon juice and a pinch of cayenne if desired. Drink immediately.

### Lentil Soup

1 lb. dry lentils

7-8 cups water

4-6 cloves garlic, minced

1 medium onion, chopped

2 stalks celery, chopped

2 carrots chopped

1 tbsp. pesto (optional; see recipe, Day 5)

8 oz. tomato sauce or 2 large tomatoes pureed in food processor (optional)

Sea salt to taste

Freshly ground black pepper

Brown-rice vinegar

1. Wash and drain lentils.
2. Place in pot with water. Bring to a boil.
3. Add garlic, onion, celery and carrots.
4. Add pesto and tomatoes if desired.
5. Reduce heat to simmer and cook until lentils are soft, approximately 1 hour.
6. Drizzle brown-rice vinegar on top of each serving. Sprinkle with black pepper.
7. Serve with crisp bread.

### Asparagus with Honey-Lemon Dressing

¾ cup tahini or peanut butter

6 tbsp. lemon juice

1 tbsp. honey

2 tsp. minced garlic

¾ cup or more water

½ tsp. fine sea salt

Pinch of cayenne pepper to taste

Fresh parsley (optional)

1¼ lbs. fresh asparagus

1 tbsp. olive oil

1. Preheat oven to 350 degrees.
2. Place tahini or peanut butter, lemon juice, honey and minced garlic in food processor. Add water and blend until desired consistency. Add salt, cayenne and parsley.
3. Rinse asparagus and break off the tough ends. Put in a baking dish. Drizzle with olive oil. Spoon dressing

over asparagus. Cover and bake for 15 minutes or until asparagus is tender.

---

## DAY 8

### Stuffed Eggplant

3 medium eggplant

2 tbsp. extra-virgin olive oil

1 small onion, chopped

8 oz. chopped mushrooms

2 cups cooked brown rice

1 tbsp. pesto (see recipe, Day 5)

½ cup grated Parmesan cheese or cubed tofu

1 cup tomato sauce (use your favorite organic variety)

1 tsp. refined sea salt (optional)

Dash of thyme

Dash of oregano

Freshly ground black pepper

4 large cloves garlic, minced

1 handful fresh parsley

1. Preheat oven to 350 degrees.
2. Cut eggplant in half lengthwise and scoop out the insides, leaving a ½-inch shell. Cut the flesh into ½-inch cubes.
3. Heat olive oil in skillet. Sauté onion and mushrooms until soft. Add rice, pesto, tofu, tomato sauce, sea salt, thyme, oregano and pepper. Cook for 3 minutes.
4. Add chopped garlic and parsley.

5.  Divide the ingredients into 6 parts and stuff eggplant shells. Sprinkle with cheese.
6.  Bake for 30 minutes.

### Tempeh, Mushrooms, and Snow Peas on a Bed of Rice

2 tbsp. olive or sesame oil

16 oz. Tempeh

3 cloves garlic, minced

1 lb. mushrooms

½ lb. snow peas

1 tsp. low-sodium tamari (optional)

2 cups cooked basmati rice

1.  In a large skillet or wok, heat oil and sauté tempeh until light brown, remove from skillet.
2.  Add mushrooms and snow peas to skillet and toss for approximately 3 minutes.
3.  Add tempeh and lightly toss.
4.  Add tamari. Serve on a bed of basmati rice.

## DAY 9

### Pasta with Cheese and Tomato Pesto Sauce

3 lbs. plum tomatoes

1 tbsp. olive oil

2 large cloves garlic

½ tsp. fennel seeds

1 tbsp. pesto (see recipe, Day 5)

2 cups cubed mozzarella cheese

1 lb. fusilli, penne, shells or other pasta

1. Puree tomatoes in a food processor. Empty into 4-qt. pot.
2. Heat oil in a skillet. Add garlic and fennel seeds and sauté until garlic is soft.
3. Add garlic and fennel mixture to tomatoes. Add pesto and cook ½ hour or until thickened.
4. Ten minutes before done, add the cubed mozzarella (tofu can be substituted).
5. Pour over cooked pasta and serve.

### Garlicky Greens

2 lbs. leafy greens, such as spinach, Swiss chard, dandelion, kale, collards, bok choy

2 tbsp. extra-virgin olive oil or toasted sesame oil

5 large cloves garlic, chopped

1 leek, chopped

1 tbsp. sesame seeds

½ tsp. tamari

1. Clean all greens. If using kale, collards, remove the ribs, spinach remove the stems.
2. In a large wok or heavy skillet, heat oil over low heat. Do not let oil smoke. Add garlic and leek and sauté until garlic is light brown.
3. Add greens and stir-fry for about 3 minutes. Add sesame seeds and stir-fry until leaves are tender.

4. Remove from heat. Add tamari and cover for about 2 minutes. Serve.

## DAY 10

### Tabouleh

1 cup bulgur wheat, rinsed

1¾ cups boiling water

¼ cup lemon juice

¼ cup extra-virgin olive oil

2 cloves garlic, minced

¼ tsp. cayenne pepper (optional)

Sea salt to taste

2 large ripe tomatoes

1 large cucumber, chopped

4 scallions, chopped

⅓ cup chopped cilantro or Italian parsley

10 chopped mint leaves (optional)

1. Combine bulgur and water in large bowl. Let stand until bulgur is tender, for about 10 minutes. Drain.
2. Add lemon juice, olive oil, garlic, cayenne and sea salt.
3. Refrigerate for at least 1 hour, then add remaining ingredients and mix well. Serve.

### Marinated Tempeh

1 lb. tempeh

1 tbsp. tamari or soy sauce

1 tsp. mirin

3 scallions, chopped

1 large clove garlic, minced

1 tbsp. toasted sesame oil

1 tbsp. kuzu (thickener)

1 tbsp. toasted sesame seeds

1. Cut tempeh into ½-inch slices and place in a saucepan.
2. Add tamari, mirin, scallions and garlic and marinate for ½ hour.
3. Remove tempeh from marinade and drain.
4. In a skillet, heat oil. Add tempeh and grill for about 5 minutes on each side.
5. Bring the marinade to a boil and add kazu to dissolve. Simmer for 1-3 minutes or until thickened.
6. Pour over tempeh. Sprinkle with sesame seeds and serve.

## DAY 11

### Sea Vegetable Salad

1 cup dried hijiki sea weed

1½ cup dried arame sea weed

½ cup chopped carrots

3 scallions, chopped

½ lb. tempeh, sautéed in tamari

1 tbsp. toasted sesame seeds

### Dressing
½ cup wheat-free tamari
½ cup organic sesame oil (or olive oil)
½ cup brown-rice vinegar
½ cup marin

1. Wash hijiki and arame in a colander for about 5 minutes. Then let soak in fresh water for ½ hour. Drain.
2. Bring 4 qts. of water to boil and add sea vegetables.
3. Simmer on low heat for approximately 30 minutes or until tender.
4. Drain and let cool.
5. Meanwhile, make dressing.
6. Add sautéed tempeh, carrots, scallions, sesame seeds and dressing to sea vegetables.
7. Toss and let stand for 30 minutes before serving.

## DAY 12

### Swiss Chard Pan Pizza
Uncooked rolled pizza dough
Dash of cornmeal
2 lbs. Swiss chard
1 tbsp. olive oil
2 cloves garlic, minced
¼ cup grated Parmesan cheese (optional)

20 pitted Kalamata olives

¼ shredded mozzarella

1. Preheat oven to 375 degrees.
2. Place rolled dough in oiled baking pan and sprinkle with cornmeal.
3. Remove the stems from the chard. Slice chard leaves in half lengthwise and then cut across the width, into one inch strips.
4. Wash chard and leave damp.
5. Heat oil in skillet and sauté garlic until light brown.
6. Add chard and sauté until tender, drain any liquid off. Spread on dough.
7. Sprinkle with Parmesan and pitted olives. Add mozzarella.
8. Bake for 40 minutes and serve.

### Chickpeas in Hot Tomato Sauce

2 cups dried chickpeas

6 cups water for cooking

1 qt. tomato basil fennel sauce (see recipe below)

1. Soak chickpeas overnight in 3 cups of water.
2. Drain and add 6 cups of fresh water. Bring to boil, then simmer for about 3 hours or until tender (you may have to add more water). Drain.
3. Add tomato sauce and simmer for 20 minutes. Cover and let stand for 15 minutes before serving.

### Tomato/Basil/Fennel Sauce

3 lbs. ripe plum tomatoes

1 tsp. olive oil

1 tsp. minced garlic

1 tsp. fennel seeds

1 tbsp. pesto (see recipe, day 5) or handful of basil leaves

1 cayenne pepper (optional)

1. In food processor chop tomatoes.
2. Heat oil in skillet and sauté garlic and fennel until garlic is light brown. Add to chopped tomatoes.
3. Add pesto or basil and cayenne.
4. Simmer until thick, 30-40 minutes.

—————————————— DAY 13 ——————————————

### Fruit Smoothie

1 frozen banana

2 oranges

1 cup organic frozen strawberries or other berries

1 cup vanilla almond or oat milk

1 tbsp. protein powder (optional)

1. Place all ingredients in a blender.
2. Mix on high speed for 20 seconds and serve.

### Lentil Salad in Pita Bread

4 cups water

2 cups dried rinsed lentils

1 bay leaf

¾ cup diced red onion

1 clove garlic, minced

½ cup diced carrots

½ cup any vegetable of your choice (optional)

6-inch strip kombu (sea vegetable)

1. In 4-qt. pot add water, lentils and bay leaf. Cover and heat to boil.
2. Soak kombu in warm water for 30 minutes. Drain, add fresh water and simmer for 20 minutes. Drain, cool and cut into ½ inch pieces. Add before serving.
3. After 10 minutes add onion, garlic, carrots, chopped vegetables and kombu.
4. Uncover and continue to boil until lentils are tender, 20-45 minutes.

### Dressing

½ cup extra-virgin olive oil

2 tbsp. lemon juice or vinegar

1½ tsp. Dijon mustard

2 cloves garlic, minced

1. Place all ingredients in small jar and shake vigorously to blend.

2. Let stand for at least 1 hour before using.
3. Refrigerate unused portion.
4. Pour dressing over salad and serve on pita bread.

——————————————— DAY 14 ———————————————

### Eggless Tofu

1 lb. organic non-GMO tofu

2 tbsp. tahini

4 tbsp. protein powder (optional)

2 tbsp. onions, chopped

½ green pepper, chopped (optional)

½ tsp. cayenne pepper

½ tsp. garlic powder or 2 cloves fresh garlic, chopped

¼ tsp. turmeric

1 tbsp. Dijon mustard

1 stalk celery, diced

1. Mash the tofu with a fork.
2. Add the remaining ingredients and mix by hand. If you prefer smoother consistency, use a blender.

### Ratatouille Over Rice

1 tbsp. olive oil

5 cloves garlic

1 tbsp. fennel seeds

1 large onion, quartered and sliced

2 cups mushrooms sliced (optional)

3 medium zucchini, cubed

2 bell peppers, chopped

1 eggplant, cubed

6-8 okra, sliced

2 cups fresh tomato sauce (see recipe, Day 9)

1. Heat oil in large skillet and sauté garlic, fennel, onion and mushrooms.
2. In a large pot add zucchini, peppers, eggplant and okra. Cook over medium heat to get some of the water out of the vegetables, stirring constantly, approximately 15 minutes.
3. Add tomato sauce and sautéed vegetables. Simmer and cook 25 minutes.
4. Turn off heat and let stand for 15 minutes before serving.

**Cucumber Tomato Salad with Chickpeas and Vinaigrette**

3 cucumbers, peeled and cubed

5 roma tomatoes, cubed in ½ inch pieces

1 can organic chickpeas, drained and rinsed

3 tbsp. olive oil

1 tsp vinegar

1 clove garlic

Dash oregano or thyme

1. Put cucumber, tomatoes, and chickpeas in a bowl.
2. Mix remaining ingredients together in separate bowl. Pour over cucumbers, tomatoes, and chickpeas.
3. Toss and let stand 30 minutes before serving.

## DAY 15

### Egg White Omelet with Mushrooms and Spinach

1 egg
5 egg whites
1 tbsp. olive oil
1 green pepper, diced (optional)
1 small zucchini diced
½ cup sliced mushrooms
¼ cup chopped spinach
3 scallions sliced (optional)
1 tsp. hing spice seasoning (aids digestion)(optional)

1. Combine egg and egg whites in a bowl and stir with a fork until well blended.
2. Heat oil in saucepan and sauté remaining ingredients.
3. Add egg mixture. Cover and cook over low flame for approximately 10 minutes or until eggs are cooked thoroughly.
4. Remove from heat and serve.

### Sautéed Brussels Sprouts

2 cups brussels sprouts, washed and cleaned, cut large ones in quarters, smaller ones in half
1 tbsp. olive oil
2 cloves garlic, minced
1 tsp. fennel seeds
Dash of tamari

1.  Steam Brussels sprouts until cooked but not soft.
2.  Heat oil in a skillet and sauté garlic with fennel seeds until garlic is light brown.
3.  Add Brussels sprouts and tamari. Cover and cook over medium heat for 5 minutes.

———————————— **DAY 16** ————————————

### Vegetable-Apple Juice Cocktail

4-5 carrots

1 apple

1 stalk celery

1.  Place ingredients in juice blender and mix.

### Zucchini Bread

3 cups flour

2 tsp. cinnamon

2 tsp. baking powder

1 tsp. baking soda

3 cups grated zucchini

3 beaten eggs (or 5 egg whites)

½ cup raw sugar

¼ cup vegetable oil or butter

1 cup walnuts chopped

1. Preheat oven to 325 degrees.
2. Mix flour, cinnamon, baking powder and baking soda in a small mixing bowl.
3. Combine zucchini, eggs, sugar and oil in a large mixing bowl and beat with fork or whisk until well blended.
4. Add the flour mixture to the zucchini-egg mixture. Add the walnuts and mix well.
5. Put into oiled and floured loaf pan and bake 1 hour.

**Cold Pasta Salad with Tomato, Basil and Mozzarella**

½ lb. pasta of choice (e.g. fusilli, penne, shells)

2 cloves garlic, minced

½ lb. firm mozzarella, (or tofu) cubed

15 fresh basil leaves

3-4 large beefsteak, or other ripe tomatoes, cubed

2 tbsp. olive oil

Black pepper and salt to taste

1. Prepare pasta.
2. While pasta is cooking, in large bowl mix garlic, cheese or tofu, basil, tomatoes and olive oil. Add pepper.
3. Mix pasta with tomato – basil mixture and refrigerate.

## DAY 17

**Tofu Chickenless Salad**

1 lb. organic GMO-free Tofu

2 tbsp. tahini

4 tbsp. nutritional yeast

2 tbsp. shallots or onions, chopped

½ tsp. cayenne pepper (optional)

¼ tsp. garlic powder, or 2 cloves fresh garlic, chopped

¼ tsp. celery seeds

1 tsp. barbecue seasoning or tamari (optional)

1 stalk celery, diced

1-3 tbsp. water (optional)

1. Put tofu in a bowl and break apart with fork.
2. Add remaining ingredients and mix. Depending on desired consistency, use a food processor. If too dry, add 1-3 tablespoons of water.

### Stir-Fried Greens with Ginger

1 lb. greens, such as spinach, or baby Swiss chard, dandelion, baby kale, baby bok choy

2 tbsp. olive oil

5 slices fresh ginger

1 leek

1. Wash all greens. Do not dry.
2. Heat oil in a large skillet or wok. Add ginger and leek and sauté until light brown.
3. Add greens and toss. Cover and cook over medium heat for 5-10 minutes or until greens are tender.

--------- DAY 18 ---------

## Garden Burger

1 lb. tofu or Quorn crumbles

1 tbsp. olive oil

1 large onion diced

1 large clove garlic

1 tsp. cumin powder

1 cup pasta sauce (use your favorite organic variety)

1 tsp. Celtic salt (optional)

½ cup toasted almonds, ground

Black pepper to taste

1 cup whole-wheat bread crumbs

1. Preheat oven to 350 degrees.
2. In a large mixing bowl, mash tofu or quorn crumbles with fork. Set aside.
3. Heat oil in skillet. Add onion, garlic and cumin and sauté until light brown.
4. Add tomato sauce and salt and simmer for 5-10 minutes.
5. Pour this mixture into bowl with crumbles. Mix.
6. Add nuts and mix. Add pepper if desired.
7. Cool mixture. Add bread crumbs and form into patties, about 3 ½ inches in diameter and ⅔ inch thick. Use extra bread crumbs if needed.
8. Bake on a lightly oiled baking sheet approximately 10 minutes on each side or until crispy.

## Marinated Shrimp and Chicken Kabobs
## With Grilled Vegetables

1 lb. raw shrimp

1 lb. boneless and skinless free-range organic chicken

1 zucchini, cut into ½-inch slices

1 mushroom

1 green pepper, cut into 1-inch pieces

1 red pepper, cut into 1-inch pieces

Prepare marinade:

¼ cup olive oil

⅛ cup vinegar

1 clove garlic, minced

dash oregano

1. Combine the marinade ingredients and pour into two separate bowls.
2. Clean and devein shrimp. Cut chicken into ¾ -inch pieces.
3. Marinate chicken and shrimp in separate bowls for 1 hour.
4. Put on skewers with vegetables.
5. Barbecue or cook under broiler until golden.

─────────── DAY 19 ───────────

## Light Vegetable Soup

2 large potatoes, diced

4 carrots, chopped

4 stalks celery, chopped

5 cloves garlic, minced

2 leeks sliced

3 large bay leaves

2 cups chopped mixed vegetables (peas, broccoli stalks, green beans)

Dash of parsley (optional)

2 cups tomato sauce (optional: see recipe, day 9)

5 cups of water

1. Combine all ingredients in a large pot and bring to a boil.
2. Reduce heat and simmer for 1 hour.
3. Let stand for 30 minutes.
4. Press vegetables through strainer into bowl with broth.
5. Let cool and refrigerate. Good for a maximum of 2 days in refrigerator, or up to 6 weeks in freezer.

### Tempeh Vegetable Stir-Fry

1 tbsp. toasted sesame oil

1 tbsp. grated fresh ginger

1 leek, chopped

1 package tempeh, cubed

1 cayenne pepper (optional)

2 large carrots, chopped

4 cups chopped washed greens, such as spinach, Swiss chard, dandelion, kale, collards, bok choy

Tamari to taste

1. Heat oil in large skillet or wok and lightly sauté ginger and leek.

2. Turn down flame and add tempeh and cayenne. Sauté until tempeh is golden.
3. Add carrots and greens, toss.
4. Cover and cook over medium heat until carrots and greens are tender. Sprinkle with water if pan is too dry.
5. Serve with tamari.

––––––––––––––––– DAY 20 –––––––––––––––––

### Couscous Salad

1 cup couscous
2 cups boiling water or seasoned vegetable broth (prepackaged)
1 tbsp. olive oil
1 clove garlic, minced
3 scallions, minced
2 carrots, chopped
½ cup thawed and rinsed frozen peas
2 cups asparagus spears, sliced in ½ inch pieces

1. Place couscous in a large serving bowl. Add boiling water or vegetable broth and stir. Cover and let sit for 10 minutes or until water is absorbed.
2. Meanwhile heat oil in a large wok or skillet. Add garlic and scallions and sauté. Add vegetables. Stir-fry vegetables until tender.
3. Plate vegetables on top of couscous and serve.

**Alternative to Couscous Salad: Quinoa Tabbouleh Salad**

½ cup quinoa

½ tsp. Celtic salt

½ tsp. ground pepper

⅓ cup tahini butter

Juice from one lemon

2 cups chopped cucumber

1 cup chopped tomato

1 cup minced parsley (may substitute with ½ cup parsley/
    ½ cup cilantro)

1. Rinse quinoa, drain. Put rinsed quinoa in saucepan, add 1 cup water to quinoa and bring to a boil. Reduce heat to low, cover and simmer for 20 minutes. Remove from heat and take off lid. Cool quinoa in pot, do not stir.
2. Mix the salt, pepper, tahini and lemon juice in a food processor.
3. In a bowl, combine quinoa, chopped vegetables, parsley and mixture from food processor; mix well. Serve.

---

## DAY 21

---

**Sautéed Greens with Sesame Seeds**

1 lb. chopped kale or collards

1 tbsp. hot sesame oil

5 slices fresh ginger

2 cloves garlic, minced

3 scallions, chopped

1 tbsp. dry roasted sesame seeds
Tamari to taste

1. Wash all greens. Do not dry.
2. Heat oil in a large skillet or wok. Add ginger, garlic and scallions and sauté lightly. Add greens and toss. Cover and let steam for 5-10 minutes or until greens are tender.
3. Add sesame seeds and tamari. Toss and let stand for 3 minutes before serving.

## RECOMMENDED BEVERAGES

| | |
|---|---|
| Green Tea | Water |
| Genmai Tea | Almond Milk |
| Kukicha Tea | Rice Milk |
| Roobois Tea | Coffee substitutes |
| Herbal Teas | Organic Coffee |
| Fresh Fruit and Vegetable Juice | Hormone-free milk |

## BREATHING AND EXERCISE PLAN

**Note:** It takes time to combine diaphragmatic breathing and exercise. When learning the exercises, stay with the ones that are comfortable and feel good to you. Never strain or push yourself until you feel uncomfortable. Choose your favorite exercises first, then expand your program as you learn each one.

## Start-up

Practice 10 minutes of diaphragmatic breathing daily. Begin to incorporate this into your day by setting a timer for every 60 minutes, so that you can remind yourself to breathe diaphragmatically. In three weeks, you will have established a healthy and sound habit of diaphragmatic breathing. When you are comfortable with diaphragmatic breathing, combine it with your exercise routine. Then move on to the 2:1 breathing practice, followed by alternate nostril breathing.

## Meditation

Begin with 5-10 minutes daily. Refer to Chapter 12 for more information.

## Optional Exercises

If you find yourself not wanting to exercise, take time to learn diaphragmatic breathing as suggested, and learn alternate nostril breathing. You can find a reputable teacher or learn the practice in *Feeling Good Matters: The Yoga of Mind, Medicine and Healing*.[1] There are also more systematic practices that can be found in this book.

PART V

Appendices

## RADIANCE DIET FOOD GUIDE

### Beans

| | |
|---|---|
| Black | Mung; split or whole |
| Chickpeas | Pinto |
| Great Northern | Soy |
| Kidney | Split peas |
| Lentil; green, red, french | Aduki |
| Lima | |

### Soy Products (organic, non-GMO only)

Miso (non-soy miso also available)

Tempeh

Tofu

Tamari

### Whole Grains

| | |
|---|---|
| Barley | Quinoa |
| Basmati rice | Rice cakes |
| Brown rice | Whole-grain crackers |
| Couscous | Whole-grain bread |
| Millet | (non-glyphosate heat) |
| Oatmeal, pre-toasted | Wild rice |

## Fruit

| | |
|---|---|
| Apricots | Lemons |
| Avocados | Mango |
| Bananas | Melons |
| Berries | Oranges |
| Dates | Peaches |
| Figs | Pears |
| Grapefruit | Pineapple |

## Vegetables

| | |
|---|---|
| Artichokes | Greens, kale, collard, beet, chard, spinach |
| Asparagus | |
| Beets | Kale |
| Bok Choy | Leeks |
| Broccoli | Lettuce, all leafy varieties |
| Brussels sprouts | Mushrooms |
| Cabbage, red and green | Mustard greens |
| Carrots | Onions |
| Celery | Peas |
| Cucumbers | Potatoes, yams |
| Dandelion greens | Shallots |
| Endive | Squash (summer and winter varieties), Butternut |
| Escarole | |
| Green beans | Zucchini |

## Nuts and Seeds

| | |
|---|---|
| Almonds | Pumpkin seeds |
| Cashews | Sesame seeds |
| Flaxseeds | Sunflower seeds |
| Pecans | Walnuts |
| Pistachios | |

## Condiments and Oils

| | |
|---|---|
| All fruit jams | Cashew butter |
| Almond butter | Ghee (clarified butter) |
| Apple butter | Honey |
| Apple cider vinegar | Peanut butter |
| Balsamic vinegar | Tahini |
| Barley malt | Tamari |
| Brown rice syrup | Cold-pressed sesame oil |
| Brown rice vinegar | Extra-virgin olive oil |
| Mirin | Peanut oil |
| Butter (organic) | Sunflower seed butter |

## Spices and Herbs

| | |
|---|---|
| Basil | Coriander, fresh, |
| Cardamom | powder and seed |
| Cinnamon | Cumin, powder and seed |
| Cloves | Fennel, fresh and seed |

Fenugreek     Oregano
Garlic     Rosemary
Ginger, fresh and powder     Sage
Hing (Asafoetida)     Thyme
Nutmeg     Turmeric
Mint

## Sea Vegetables

Agar-agar     Kombu (kelp)
Arame     Shiitake
Dulse     Wakame
Hijiki

## Beverages

Green Tea     Water
Genmai Tea     Almond Milk
Kukicha Tea     Rice Milk
Roobois Tea     Coffee substitutes
Herbal Teas     Organic Coffee
Fresh Fruit and     Hormone-free milk
    Vegetable Juice

## COMMON ESSENTIAL OILS
(Not to Be Ingested)

**Basil:** One of the best aromatic nerve tonics. Used to relieve mental fatigue due to stress.

**Chamomile:** Relieves stress by relaxing the body and calming the nerves.

**Clary Sage:** Use as a tonic for the nervous system.

**Cypress:** Astringent. Use in combination with juniper to tone muscles.

**Jasmine:** Elevates mood. It's commonly used as an aphrodisiac.

**Juniper:** One of the most versatile oils. Has many properties, one being a diuretic. Use in combination with cypress to help decrease cellulite.

**Lavender:** Reduces stress and relieves headaches.

**Neroli:** Among the finest flower oils. Acts to renew cells. Makes a luxurious and relaxing bath or massage oil.

**Rose:** The quintessential scent of romance. Uplifts your spirit.

**Rosemary:** Nervous system stimulant. Produces clarity of mind.

**Sandalwood:** Use to relax and calm the mind and body. Excellent when combined with other oils.

**Ylang-ylang:** Aphrodisiac. Called the flower of flowers. One of the most emotionally evocative essential oils.

# ESSENTIAL OIL RECIPES

## Thigh Enhancer

Juniper (1-2 drops in bath), cypress (1-2 drops in bath), and lavender (1-2 drops in bath). *Those troubled with cellulite due to fluid retention will find this useful and relaxing.*

## Tension Reliever

Lavender. *One drop on temples will enhance sleep and relieve headache due to stress.*

## Stress Buster

Neroli (3 drops in bath). *Eases tension and stress. Aids in sleep. Mixes well with lavender.*

## Mental Rejuvenator

Juniper, rosemary, and basil. *Mix 5 drops of each, in 30 ml. of oil. Massage on temples to promote alertness.*

## Sensuality Stimulant

Ylang-Ylang. As a massage oil, must be diluted, so add 5 drops to 10ml. of oil. As a bath oil, add 4 drops, and 2 drops of sandalwood to bath.

## Menstrual Pain Reliever

Lavender (4 drops), chamomile (3 drops), and clary sage (3 drops). Mix into 10ml. almond oil. Rub over abdomen and lower back.

## NORTH AMERICAN FLOWER ESSENCES
## FOR RADIANCE

**Aloe Vera:** Rejuvenates the body, and redirects creative forces.

**Alpine Lily:** Enhances vital female energy.

**Arnica:** Repairs life energy after shock or trauma.

**California Wild Rose:** Helps reduce anxiety.

**Crab Apple:** Eases feelings of shame.

**Easter Lily:** Relieves congested energy.

**Evening Primrose:** Helps reconnect with intimacy.

**Hibiscus:** Helps connect with one's female sexuality.

**Lady's Slipper:** Helps with sexual depletion. Balances lower chakras.

**Mariposa Lily:** Helps to restore feeling nourished and secure.

**Morning Glory:** Revitalizes energy.

**Mountain Pride:** Stimulates assertiveness.

**Olive:** Reinvigorates energy after physical exertion.

**Pink Monkey Flower:** Eases feelings of unworthiness and shame.

**Pretty Face:** Increases sense of physical beauty.

**Queen Anne's Lace:** Transforms sexuality into spirituality. Integrates lower and higher chakras.

**Self-Heal:** Promotes a vital sense of self.

**Snapdragon:** Helps develop a strong libido.

**Sticky Monkey Flower:** Helps express sexual feelings.

**Yarrow:** When taken with Echinacea and Arnica protects against harmful environmental influences.

Appendices

# FLOWER ESSENCE RECIPE

**Note:** Since flower essence formulas are created according to your personal needs, I included only one recipe (essences are available online) helpful for women's rejuvenation.

## Rejuvenation

In 1 oz. of distilled water, add:

2 drops of brandy (preservative)

2 drops of *Bach*: Crab Apple, Gorse, Hornbeam, Olive;

2 drops of *Himalayan*: Lotus, Peacock Flower

4 drops of *Australian Bush*: Macrocarpa, Spinifex

*Mix the above combination of flower essences. Add 2 drops of this mixture to water and sip throughout the day.*

If you want to experiment with additional recipes with the help of a practitioner or on your own, I recommend using a good reference book. There are a few great books you can buy online:

- *Flower Essence Repertory*: by Patricia Kaminski and Richard Katz
- *The Bach Flower Remedies*: by Edward Bach
- *Bach Flower Therapy, Theory and Practice*: by Mechthild Scheffer
- *Healing with Flower Essences*: by Joan Greenblatt
- *Australian Bush Flower Essences*: by Ian White
- *The New Encyclopedia of Flower Remedies*: by Clare G. Harvey

# TEN COOKING HERBS THAT
# IGNITE METABOLISM

| | |
|---|---|
| Black peppercorns | Cumin |
| Cardamom | Fennel |
| Cayenne pepper | Garlic |
| Cinnamon | Ginger |
| Coriander | Turmeric |

# HERBAL ALLIES

**Ashwagandha:** Ashwagandha is used as an "adaptogen" to help the body cope with daily stress, improves thinking ability, decreases pain and swelling (inflammation), and prevents the effects of aging.

**Brahmi (Bacopa monnieri):** An important brain tonic in Ayurvedic medicine. Nourishes the nervous system, boosts brain function, and is neuroprotective.

**Chaste Tree (VITEX):** Nourishes the mucous membrane. Promotes progesterone.

**Dandelion:** Mover of blood and lymph. Regulates sex hormones.

**Dong Quai:** Called "female ginseng." Regulates hormones.

**Ginger:** Regulates the eicosanoids, which balance metabolism.

**Ginkgo:** Stimulates blood flow to brain and extremities.

**Gotu Kola (Centella asiatica):** An important brain tonic in Ayurvedic medicine. Supports mental clarity, memory and focus.

**Licorice:** Contains estriol and isoflavone, which act as rejuvenators of the endocrine system.

**Milk thistle:** Strengthens liver and protects against environmental toxins.

**Oat straw** (Avena sativa): Nourishes nervous and endocrine systems. **Siberian Ginseng:** Rejuvenates adrenals and nervous system.

**St. John's Wort:** Mood elevator. Relieves depression and anxiety.

**Turmeric:** Regulates hormone function and promotes proper metabolism.

**Wild Yam:** Good source of zinc.

## NUTRIENTS FOR VITALITY

**Vitamin A:** Antioxidant. Restores decreased thyroid levels. (toxic in high doses)

**B-complex:** Contributes to production of sex hormones and to thyroid function.

**Beta-carotene:** Supports mucus membranes.

**Bioflavonoids:** Supports cell membranes.

**Vitamin C:** Antioxidant. Strengthens cells walls and enhances activity of enzyme pathways. Required for progesterone secretion.

**Calcium:** Benefits nervous system and healthy bone function.

**Magnesium:** Activates enzymes to metabolize amino acids and promotes utilization of other vitamins in maintaining acid/base balance.

**Selenium:** Antioxidant. Helps protect the body from environmental toxins. Good for thyroid, which affects metabolism.

**Zinc:** Vital for proper functioning of sex glands. Good for thyroid function and increased sex drive.

## WOMEN'S NOURISHERS
(Remember: The best rejuvenative is the mind.)

| | |
|---|---|
| Asparagus | Garlic |
| Cloves | Ginseng |
| Damiana | Hibiscus |
| Dong quai | Onion |
| Fenugreek | Wild yam |
| Fo-ti | |

## WOMEN'S DAILY REJUVENATING TONIC

½ tsp. licorice root powder
½ tsp. cardamom seeds
1 slice fresh ginger
Dash of cinnamon

*Mix in one quart boiling water. Let steep for thirty to forty five minutes, then strain and ingest.*

# ADDITIONAL RESOURCES FOR
# FURTHER STUDY

## AYURVEDA

Frawley, D. (2000). *Ayurvedic Healing: A Comprehensive Guide* (2nd rev. and enl. ed.). Twin Lakes, WI. Lotus Press.

Frawley, D. and Vasant, L. (1986) *The Yoga of Herbs.* Twin Lakes, WI. Lotus Press.

Frawley, D. (1997). *Ayurveda and the Mind: The Healing of Consciousness.* Twin Lakes, WI. Lotus Press.

Lad, V. (1984) *Ayurveda: The Science of Self-Healing.* Santa Fe, NM. Lotus Press.

Svoboda, R. (1999). *Ayurveda for Women: A Guide to Vitality and Health.* Devon, England. David & Charles.

Svoboda, R. (1989). *Prakruti: Your Ayurvedic Constitution.* Albuquerque, NM. GEOCOM.

Welch, C. (2011). *Balance your Hormones, Balance your Life: Achieving Optimal Health and Wellness Through Ayurveda, Chinese Medicine, and Western Science.* Cambridge, MA. Da Capo Lifelong Books.

## TRADITIONAL CHINESE MEDICINE

Beinfield, H. & Korngold, E. (1992). *Between Heaven and Earth: A Guide to Chinese Medicine.* New York. Ballantine Books.

Beinfield, H. & Korngold, E. (1992). *A Guide to Chinese Medicine.* New York. Ballantine Books.

Hammer, L. (1991). *Dragon Rises, Red Bird Flies: Psychology, Energy & Chinese Medicine.* Barrytown, NY, Station Hill Press.

Kaptchuk, T. (1983). *The Web that Has No Weaver: Understanding Chinese Medicine.* New York. Congdon & Weed.

Veith, I. (1972). *Huang Ti nei ching su wên. The Yellow Emperor's Classic of Internal Medicine.* Chapters 1-34 (New edition). Berkeley, CA. University of California Press.

## HOLISTIC HEALTH & NUTRITION

Ballentine, R. (2011). *Radical Healing: Integrating the World's Great Therapeutic Traditions to Create a New Transformative Medicine.* Honesdale, PA. Himalayan Institute Press.

Bland, J. (2014). *The Disease Delusion: Conquering the Causes of Chronic Illness for a Healthier, Longer, and Happier Life.* New York. Harper Wave.

Campbell, T. & Campbell, T. (2005). *The China Study: The Most Comprehensive Study of Nutrition Ever Conducted and the Startling Implications for Diet, Weight Loss and Long-Term Health.* Dallas, TX. BenBella Books.

Fallon, S. & Enig, M. (2001). *Nourishing Traditions: The Cookbook That Challenges Politically Correct Nutrition and the Diet Dictocrats* (2nd rev. edition). Washington, D.C. New Trends Pub.

Gershon, M. (1998). *The Second Brain: The Scientific Basis of Gut. Instinct and a Groundbreaking New Understanding of Nervous Disorders of the Stomach and Intestine.* New York, NY. Harper Collins.

Greenblatt, J. (2011) *Healing with Flower Essences: How to Use Natural Botanicals for Spiritual and Emotional Well-Being.* Carlsbad, CA. Aperion Books.

Greenblatt, J. (2012) *A Culinary Journey: A Personal Voyage Into the World of Herbs, Spices & Vegetarian Cuisine.* Carlsbad, CA. Aperion Books.

Haas, E., & Levin, B. (2006). *Staying Healthy with Nutrition: The Complete Guide to Diet and Nutritional Medicine* (21st-century edition). Berkeley, CA. Celestial Arts.

Lipton, B. (2005). *The Biology of Belief: Unleashing the Power of Consciousness, Matter and Miracles.* Santa Rosa, CA. Mountain of Love/Elite Books.

Pert, C. (1997). *Molecules of Emotion: Why You Feel the Way You Feel.* New York, NY: Scribner.

Price, W. and Price P. (2009) *Nutrition and Physical Degeneration.* (8th edition).

Taylor, S. (2015). *Feeling Good Matters: The Yoga of Mind, Medicine and Healing.* PA. CMS.

Taylor, S. (2007). *The Vital Energy Program.* CD Set. Sounds True.

Taylor, S. (1998). *Sexual Radiance: A 21-Day Program of Breathwork, Nutrition, and Exercise for Vitality and Sensuality.* New York: Harmony Books.

Weed, S. (2002). *New Menopausal Years: The Wise Woman Way.* Woodstock, NY. Ash Tree Pub.

## YOGA & MEDITATION

Anderson, S. (2007). *Yoga: Mastering the Basics.* Honesdale, PA: Himalayan Institute Press.

Coulter, H. (2001). *Anatomy of Hatha Yoga: A Manual for Students, Teachers, and Practitioners.* Marlboro, VT. Body and Breath, Inc.

Frawley, D. (1999). *Yoga and Ayurveda: Self-Healing and Self-Realization.* Twin Lakes, WI. Lotus Light Pub.

Iyengar, B. (1979). *Light on Yoga: Yoga Dipika.* (rev. [pbk.] edition). New York: Schocken Books.

Kaminoff, L. & Matthews, A. (2011). *Yoga Anatomy.* (2nd edition). *Champaign, IL: Human Kinetics.* Long, R. & Macivor, C. (2008). *The Key Poses of Yoga: Your Guide to Functional Anatomy in Yoga.* (2nd Vol.). Canada. Bandha Yoga.

Pandit Rajmani Tigunait (2014). *The Secret of the Yoga Sutras.* Honesdale, PA. Himalayan Institute Press.

Pandit Rajmani Tigunait (2019) *Vishoka Meditation: The Yoga of Inner Radiance.* Honesdale, PA. The Himalyan Institute Press.

Swami Rama (1984). *Exercise Without Movement.* Honesdale, PA. Himalayan Institute Press.

Swami Rama (1982). *Joints and Glands Exercises: As Taught By Sri Swami Rama of the Himalayas.* (2nd edition). Honesdale, PA. Himalayan International Institute.

Swami Muktibodhananda Saraswati (1985). *Hatha Yoga Pradipika.* Munger, Bihar, India. Bihar School of Yoga.

# Appendices

## HOLISTIC PSYCHOLOGY

Eknath, E. (2010). *Conquest of Mind: Take Charge of Your Thoughts and Reshape your Life Through Meditation* (3rd rev. edition). New York. Nilgiri Press.

Eknath, E. (2010). *Patience: A Little Book of Inner Strength*. New York. Nilgiri Press.

Harish, Johari (1989). *Breath, Mind, and Consciousness*. Rochester, VT. Destiny Books.

Lama, Dalai (2012). *The Mind's Own Physician: A Scientific Dialogue with the Dalai Lama on the Healing Power of Meditation*. Oakland, CA. New Harbinger Publications.

Swami Rama (1982). *Creative Use of Emotion*. Honesdale, PA. Himalayan Institute Press.

Swami Rama, Ballentine, R., Swami Ajaya (1976). *Yoga and Psychotherapy: The Evolution of Consciousness*. Honesdale, PA. Himalayan Institute Press.

Swami Ajaya (1982). *Yoga Psychology: A Practical Guide to Meditation*. Honesdale, PA. Himalayan Institute Press.

Trungpa, C. & Gimian, C. (1984). *Shambhala: The Sacred Path of the Warrior*. Boulder, CO. Shambhala Publications.

Tulku, Thondup (1996). *The Healing Power of Mind: Simple Meditation Exercises for Health, Well-Being, and Enlightenment*. Boston, MA. Shambhala Publications.

## OTHER

Buhner, S. (2002). *The Lost Language of Plants: The Ecological Importance of Plant Medicines to Life on Earth.* White River Junction, VT. Chelsea Green Pub.

Doidge, N. (2007). *The Brain That Changes Itself: Stories of Personal Triumph From the Frontiers of Brain Science.* New York. Penguin.

Feldenkrais, M. (1990). *Awareness Through Movement: Easy-to-Do Health Exercises to Improve Your Posture, Vision, Imagination, and Personal Awareness.* New York. Harper One.

Pearce, J. (1992). *Evolution's End: Claiming the Potential of Our Intelligence.* San Francisco, CA. HarperSanFrancisco.

Tompkins, P. & Bird, C. (1973). *The Secret Life of Plants.* New York. Harper & Row.

Appendices

# REFERENCES

**Chapter 2**

1. Xie et al "Sleep initiated fluid flux drives metabolite clearance from the adult brain." *Science*, October 18, 2013. DOI: 10.1126/science.1241224.

2. Cenini, Giovanna, and Wolfgang Voos. "Mitochondria as Potential Targets in Alzheimer Disease Therapy: An Update." Frontiers in Pharmacology 10 (2019). https://doi.org/10.3389/fphar.2019.00902.

3. Tsai, Pei-I, Chin-Hsien Lin, Chung-Han Hsieh, Amanda M Papakyrikos, Min Joo Kim, Valerio Napolioni, Carmen Schoor, et al. "PINK1 Phosphorylates MIC60/Mitofilin to Control Structural Plasticity of Mitochondrial Crista Junctions" *Molecular cell* 69, no. 5 (2018): 744-756.e6. doi: 10.1016/j.molcel.2018.01.026.

4. Almario, Christopher V., Megana L. Ballal, William D. Chey, Carl Nordstrom, Dinesh Khanna, and Brennan M. R. Spiegel. "Burden of Gastrointestinal Symptoms in the United States: Results of a Nationally Representative Survey of Over 71,000 Americans." American Journal of Gastroenterology 113, no. 11 (2018): 1701–10. https://doi.org/10.1038/s41395-018-0256-8.

5. "Dietary Guidelines." ChooseMyPlate. US Department of Agriculture, 2015. Accessed. April 5, 2020. https://www.choosemyplate.gov/eathealthy/dietary-guidelines.

6. Russo MA, Santarelli DM, O'Rourke D. (2017), "The physiological effects of slow breathing in the healthy human." *Breathe* (Sheffield England). 13,4:298-309. doi: 10.1183/20734735.009817.

7. Shibata, S., Fujimoto, N., Hastings, J.L., Carrick-Ranson, G., Bhella, P.S., Hearon, C.M., Jr. and Levine, B.D. (2018), "The effect of lifelong exercise frequency on arterial stiffness." *J Physiol*, 596: 2783-2795. https://doi.org/10.1113/JP275301.

**Chapter 3**

1. Sakatani, Kaoru. "Concept of Mind and Brain in Traditional Chinese Medicine." Data Science Journal 6 (2007). https://doi.org/10.2481/dsj.6.s220.

2. S. Taylor, *Feeling Good Matters: The Yoga of Mind, Medicine and Healing.* (Pennsylvania: CMS Press, 2015).

3. Bodsworth, Jon. "Weighing the Heart, Book of the Dead." *Ancient History Encyclopedia.* Last modified April 26, 2012.

4. I. Veith, *The Yellow Emperor's Classic of Internal Medicine.* (Berkeley: University of California Press, 1966).

5. P. Kaminski & R. Katz, *Flower Essence Repertory: A Comprehensive Guide to North American and English Flower Essences for Emotional and Spiritual Well-Being.* (Nevada: Flower Essence Society, 1994).
6. Hill DA, Artis D. Intestinal bacteria and the regulation of immune cell homeostasis. *Annu Rev Immunol.* (2010) 28:623–67. doi: 10.1146/annurev-immunol-030409-101330.
7. Bellavite P, Conforti A, Piasere V, Ortolani R. Immunology and homeopathy. 1. Historical background. *Evid Based Complement Alternat Med.* (2005) 2:441–52.
8. Duffy LC, Zielezny MA, Marshall JR, et al. Relevance of major stress events as an indicator of disease activity prevalence in inflammatory bowel disease. *Behav Med.* (1991)17:101–110.
9. Ader, R., N. Cohen, and D. Felten. "Psychoneuroimmunology: Interactions between the Nervous System and the Immune System." The Lancet 345, no. 8942 (1995): 99–103. https://doi.org/10.1016/s0140-6736(95)90066-7.
10. Ader, Robert. Psychoneuroimmunology. Amsterdam: Elsevier Academic Press, 2007.
11. Živković, Irena, Ana Rakin, Danica Petrović-Djergović, Biljana Miljković, and Mileva Mićić. "The Effects of Chronic Stress on Thymus Innervation in the Adult Rat." Acta Histochemica 106, no. 6 (2005): 449–58. https://doi.org/10.1016/j.acthis.2004.11.002.
12. Richter M., Wright, R.A. (2013) "Parasympathetic Nervous System (PNS)." In: Gellman M.D., Turner J.R. (eds) *Encyclopedia of Behavioral Medicine.* Springer, New York, NY.
13. Hekimi, Siegfried, Jérôme Lapointe, and Yang Wen. "Taking a 'Good' Look at Free Radicals in the Aging Process." *Trends in Cell Biology* 21, no. 10 (2011): 569–76. https://doi.org/10.1016/j.tcb.2011.06.008.
14. Giarman, N., Freedman, D. & Picard-ami, L. "Serotonin Content of the Pineal Glands of Man and Monkey," *Nature* 186, 480–481 (1960). https://doi.org/10.1038/186480a0.
15. Jewett BE, Sharma S. Physiology, GABA. [Updated 2019 Mar 14]. In: StatPearls [Internet]. Treasure Island (FL): StatPearls Publishing. January 2020. https://www.ncbi.nlm.nih.gov/books/NBK513311/
16. 114 W.M. Kenkel,. & C.S. Carter. "Voluntary exercise facilitates pair-bonding in male prairie voles." *Behavioral Brain Research*, 296 (Jan. 1, 2016): 326-330. Doi: 10.1016/j.bbr.2015.09.028. PMID: 26409174.

# Appendices

## Chapter 4

1. Cardinali, Daniel P., Analia M. Furio, and Luis I. Brusco. "Clinical Aspects of Melatonin Intervention in Alzheimer's Disease Progression." Current Neuropharmacology 8, no. 3 (January 2010): 218–27. https://doi.org/10.2174/157015910792246209, accessed April 3, 2020.
2. Barton, Debra L., Lynne T. Shuster, Travis Dockter, Pamela J. Atherton, Jacqueline Thielen, Stephen N. Birrell, Richa Sood, et al. "Systemic and Local Effects of Vaginal Dehydroepiandrosterone (DHEA): NCCTG N10C1 (Alliance)." Supportive Care in Cancer 26, no. 4 (November 21, 2017): 1335–43. https://doi.org/10.1007/s00520-017-3960-9.
3. G. Enders, Gut: The Inside Story of Our Body's Most Underrated. Organ. (Vancouver, BC Canada: Greystone Books, 2018), 29.
4. Mason, Peggy. "Enteric Nervous System - Neural Communication Embodied Emotion." Coursera. Michigan State University, April 6, 2020. http://www.coursera.org/lecture/neurobiology/enteric-nervous-system-kHpW6.
5. Baker, Michael E. "Flavonoids as Hormones." Advances in Experimental Medicine and Biology Flavonoids in the Living System, 1998, 249–67. https://doi.org/10.1007/978-1-4615-5335-9_18.

## Chapter 5

1. Swami S. Saraswati & Swami N. Saraswati, Prana Vidya. (Munger, India: Yoga Publications Trust, 2013), 3.
2. Ibid.
3. V. Lad. and A. Durve, Marma Points of Ayurveda: The Energy Pathways for Healing Body, Mind and Consciousness with Comparison to Traditional Chinese Medicine. (Albuquerque, New Mexico: The Ayurvedic Press, 2015), 29.
4. Ibid.
5. Johnson, Linda. March 25, 2020. https://yogainternational.com/article/view/the-koshas-5-layers-of-being,
6. Ibid
7. Ibid.
8. Ibid.
9. Ibid.

## Chapter 6

1. "Resilience Training - Evidence-Based Training to Build Resilience." DrSusanTaylor.com, October 27, 2018. https://drsusantaylor.com/resilience-training/

2. P. R. Tigunait, "Living Tantra." Study And Download Yoga Online. Yoga International, April 2010. https://yogainternational.com/ecourse/living-tantra.
3. S. Taylor, *Feeling Good Matters: The Yoga of Mind, Medicine and Healing.* (Pennsylvania: CMS Press, 2015).

**Chapter 7**
1. J. Harish, *Breath, Mind, and Consciousness.* Destiny Books; Original ed. edition (November 1, 1989).
2. Kadohisa, Mikiko. "Effects of Odor on Emotion, with Implications." *Frontiers in Systems Neuroscience* 7 (October 10, 2013). https://doi.org/10.3389/fnsys.2013.00066.
3. D. Frawley, *Ayurvedic Healing: A Comprehensive Guide.* Twin Lakes, Wisconsin: Lotus Press, 2000).
4. S. Taylor, *Sexual Radiance: A 21-Day Program for Vitality and Sensuality.* (New York: Crown Publishing, 1998).

**Chapter 9**
1. S. Taylor, *Sexual Radiance: A 21-Day Program for Vitality and Sensuality.* (New York: Crown Publishing, 1998).
2. Wegman, Martin P., Michael H. Guo, Douglas M. Bennion, Meena N. Shankar, Stephen M. Chrzanowski, Leslie A. Goldberg, Jinze Xu, et al. "Practicality of Intermittent Fasting in Humans and Its Effect on Oxidative Stress and Genes Related to Aging and Metabolism." *Rejuvenation Research* 18, no. 2 (April 18, 2015): 162–72. https://doi.org/10.1089/rej.2014.1624,
3. S. Taylor, *Feeling Good Matters: The Yoga of Mind, Medicine and Healing.* (Pennsylvania: CMS Press, 2015).
4. P. Kaminski & R. Katz, *Flower Essence Repertory: A Comprehensive Guide to North American and English Flower Essences for Emotional and Spiritual Well-Being.* (Nevada: Flower Essence Society, 1994).
5. "Are Essential Oils Safe?" Taking Charge of Your Health & Wellbeing. May 8, 2020. https://www.takingcharge.csh.umn.edu/explore-healing-practices/aromatherapy/are-essential-oils-safe.
6. "How to Use Essential Oils Effectively." Floracopeia. May 8, 2020. https://www.floracopeia.com/how-to-use-essential-oils-effectively.
7. "Are Essential Oils Safe?" Taking Charge of Your Health & Wellbeing. May 8, 2020. https://www.takingcharge.csh.umn.edu/explore-healing-practices/aromatherapy/are-essential-oils-safe.

# Appendices

**Chapter 11**
1. Donnelly, Joseph E., Steven N. Blair, John M. Jakicic, Melinda M. Manore, Janet W. Rankin, and Bryan K. Smith. "Appropriate Physical Activity Intervention Strategies for Weight Loss and Prevention of Weight Regain for Adults." *Medicine & Science in Sports & Exercise* 41, no. 2 (2009): 459–71. https://doi.org/10.1249/mss.0b013e3181949333.
2. M. Feldenkrais, Awareness through Movement: Easy-to-Do Health Exercises to Improve Your Posture, Vision, Imagination, and Personal Awareness. New York: HarperOne, 1990.

**Chapter 12**
1. "America's #1 Health Problem." The American Institute of Stress, January 4, 2017. https://www.stress.org/americas-1-health-problem.
2. "Mental Disorders Affect One in Four People." World Health Organization. World Health Organization, July 29, 2013. https://www.who.int/whr/2001/media_centre/press_release/en/.
3. "Facts and Figures." Alzheimer's Disease and Dementia. April 6, 2020. https://www.alz.org/alzheimers-dementia/facts-figures.
4. Kang, Do-Hyung, Hang Joon Jo, Wi Hoon Jung, Sun Hyung Kim, Ye-Ha Jung, Chi-Hoon Choi, Ul Soon Lee, Seung Chan An, Joon Hwan Jang, and Jun Soo Kwon. "The Effect of Meditation on Brain Structure: Cortical Thickness Mapping and Diffusion Tensor Imaging." *Social Cognitive and Affective Neuroscience* 8, no. 1 (July 2012): 27–33. https://doi.org/10.1093/scan/nss056,
5. P.R. Tigunait, *Vishoka Meditation: The Yoga of Inner Radiance.* (Pennsylvania: The Himalyan Institute Press, 2019).

**Part 4 Start-Up Plan**
1. S. Taylor, *Feeling Good Matters: The Yoga of Mind, Medicine and Healing.* (Pennsylvania: CMS Press, 2015).

# About the Author

Understanding the link between psychological function and physical reality has been a life-long commitment for Susan Taylor. This passion for knowing how the mind-body matrix plays a role in our health and healing mechanisms began at Columbia University Medical School, Institute of Nutrition, where Susan Taylor earned a master's degree. It became the foundation for her clinical nutrition practice in which she specialized in the nutrient factors that affect psychological function.

As her career unfolded, Dr. Taylor honed her skills through client and workshop sessions that concentrated on resolving physical, emotional, and psychological issues related to diet and nutrition. Subsequently, she received a PhD from Case Western Reserve University School of Medicine, where she conducted research in Nutritional Biochemistry that appeared in *The American Journal of Physiology, Analytical Biochemistry* and *Clinica Chimica Acta*.

For more than 25 years, Susan has gained international renown as a teacher concentrating on *stress related health issues*. Her unique approach blends the healing protocols of Ayurvedic Nutrition, Traditional Chinese Medicine and evidence-based meditation, and emphasizes practical ways to integrate the best of Western Medicine with natural healing traditions.

She developed the widely acclaimed "Meditation Specialist Program," which provides skills-building competency training that leads to certification for a diverse range of healthcare specialists. It is one of the most comprehensive training currently available in the science of meditation and its practices. During the past 18 years, she established the Center for Meditation Science, which offers national and international programs for healthcare practitioners, the Department of Defense, teachers, business professionals, and those interested in nutrition and meditation for self-transformation. She is acknowledged for her work in meditation and mindfulness in the Journal of Clinical Psychopharmacology.

Susan Taylor has authored several publications that include, *Feeling Good Matters: The Yoga of Mind, Medicine, and Healing, The Vital Energy Program, Sexual Radiance, Focused Awareness Meditation Guide*, and *The Healing Power of Meditation* CD series. Taylor hosts a weekly podcast on "Mind, Medicine and Healing."